Inventing the Future: the 1723 Constitutions

Ric Berman

The Old Stables Press
• Oxfordshire •
2022

The Old Stables Press, Goring Heath, Oxon., RG8 7RT UK.
First published 2022.
theoldstablespress@gmail.com

British Library Cataloguing in Publication Data
A CIP catalogue record for this book is available from the British Library

Library of Congress Cataloguing-in-Publication Data
Berman, Ric
Inventing the Future: the 1723 Constitutions /Ric Berman
p. cm.

ISBN: 978-0-9957568-9-2

1. English History
2. Masonic History
3. Philosophy - Ethics & Moral Philosophy

Inventing the Future:
the 1723 Constitutions

Other Titles by the Author

The Foundations of Modern Freemasonry –
The Grand Architects: Political Change and the
Scientific Enlightenment, 1714-1740

Schism: the Battle that Forged Freemasonry

Foundations - new light on the formation and early years of The Grand Lodge of England

Espionage, Diplomacy & the Lodge -
Charles Delafaye and the Secret Department of the Post Office

From Roanoke to Raleigh:
Freemasonry in North Carolina, 1730-1800

Loyalists & Malcontents:
Freemasonry & Revolution in South Carolina and Georgia

The Grand Lodge of England & Colonial America:
America's Grand Masters

CONSTITUTIONS 1723

If anyone doubts that Freemasonry as it is practised today was derived from the Grand Lodge of England, let him compare the new Charges with those of an older date. He will find that the severance from any and all pre-existing connections was as fundamental and complete as was the severance of the American colonies from England after the adoption of the Declaration of Independence...

The history of Freemasonry begins with a declaration of principles. These are set forth in the New Constitutions promulgated by the Grand Lodge of England and form the basic law of the Fraternity throughout the world. Indeed, the story of Freemasonry is merely the working out of those principles.

Ossian Lang,
History of Freemasonry in the State of New York
(New York, 1922)

CONTENTS

Page

Anthony Sayer
The first Grand Master of the Grand Lodge of England.
Copy of a portrait by Joseph Highmore (1692-1780)
by Thomas Richard Hinks Beaumont (1857-1940)

SUMMARY & INTRODUCTION

The 1723 *Constitutions of the Freemasons* were a product of their time and of the authors' values and beliefs. Perhaps key to understanding this context is an appreciation of the febrile political and religious nature of the early decades of the eighteenth century, a period marked by the political fallout from the death of Queen Anne, the last of the Stuart monarchs, and the coronation two months later of Prince George of Hanover as George I of Britain.

A large minority comprising those who supported James Stuart, 'the Pretender''s claim to the throne, a combination of Catholics, Non-Jurors and Tories, were opposed to George I, and his accession in October 1714 was followed by riots in towns and cities from Canterbury to Shrewsbury and Taunton to Norwich. London was not immune. The king's return from the Lord Mayor's banquet the following month was disrupted by protesters, while rioting broke out at Whitechapel.

Taking advantage of the discontent and building on an existing support base, the Earl of Mar raised James Stuart's royal standard at Braemar the following year in the hope of fomenting rebellion: the 1715 Jacobite Rising. He met with initial success and a swathe of Scotland went over to 'the king over the water' – 'the Pretender', as did much of the border counties of Cumberland, Northumberland and Durham.

The Jacobite insurrection was a product of several factors, not just the coronation of George I, including lingering Scottish resentment at the corruption that accompanied the passing of the Act of Union by the Scottish Parliament just eight years earlier. Members of the Scottish aristocracy had been bribed with cash and honours and Robert Burns' castigating comment that Scotland had been 'bought and sold for English gold' reflected the political reality.

Other factors were equally important. Although James Stuart was the late queen's half-brother and thus her closest living relative, as a Catholic he was excluded from succeeding by the Act of Settlement which limited future monarchs to James I's Protestant heirs alone. The roots of this legislation lay in the England's religious civil war, which was arguably part of a Europe-wide conflict between Catholicism and Protestantism, and in the 'Glorious Revolution' of 1688 which led to the expulsion of James II. That was followed in 1689 by a Bill of Rights drawn up by Parliament and agreed by William and Mary, which ushered in a constitutional as opposed to an absolute monarchy. The Act of Settlement reinforced this and ensured a Protestant succession to the throne.

But despite this and for reasons discussed below, many in Britain remained unreconciled to the exclusion of James Stuart and what was seen as his divine right to be crowned king.

Similarly worrying for the British government were James's other political allies, France, Spain and Sweden, who for different reasons were willing to offer tangible assistance to James's 'Jacobite' supporters in their quest to replace George I.

Consequently, putting down the 1715 Rising did not destroy the Jacobite opposition and successive British governments feared with reason that a French or Spanish-backed invasion in tandem with another uprising would decimate Hanoverian Britain: George I would be deposed; his Whig government dismissed; and the political clock dialled back forty years with the crowning of James Stuart and the return of an absolutist Catholic monarch.

Such concerns were genuine, shared widely, and largely justified, in part if not in whole. Within the following five years there would be three more attempts to destabilise Britain: 1717, 1719 and 1721.

The dates are significant, the first coinciding with the formation of the first Grand Lodge of England and the last with the installation of the Duke of Montagu as its first noble Grand

Master. This was not a coincidence. During the 1720s Grand Lodge moved to provide support for the Hanoverian status quo. In particular, its new Constitutions embodied the philosophical principles that lay behind the 'Glorious Revolution' of 1688 and the 1689 Bill of Rights, and through the influence of the Duke of Montagu, the Duke of Richmond, Dr Jean Theophilus Desaguliers, George Payne, and others, Freemasonry was transformed into an organisation that advanced a modernist Enlightenment agenda, championed aspiration and opposed absolutism.

These ideas, radical at the time, are explained in detail below.

* * * *

The transformation of Freemasonry at the beginning of the eighteenth century was effected through the introduction of new Masonic ritual and the rewriting of Freemasonry's Charges and Regulations to advance principles that included constitutional government; religious tolerance; the promotion of education and science – a world interpreted through rational observation rather than religious diktat; meritocracy; and democratic accountability.

The change was driven in part by an émigré French Protestant – a Huguenot – Jean Theophilus Desaguliers, one of the most influential figures within the inner circle of Grand Lodge. The Huguenots had fled persecution in France in their tens of thousands from the mid-1680s through to the early 1700s. An estimated 50-80,000 lived in London alone, around 10% of the capital's population.

They had been hounded and harassed for their faith and deprived of their civil liberties in France and having found sanctuary in England the Huguenots became among the most patriotic of Britons and fervent supporters of George I, whom they saw as a bulwark against Louis XIV and Louis XV.

In common with other émigrés, the Huguenots were motivated, educated, and willing to assimilate. Many embraced Freemasonry which gained stature as a beacon for the aspirational within society as it promoted leading-edge philosophical principles.

Within barely a decade of the establishment of the Grand Lodge of England in 1717, Freemasonry had become the largest and unarguably the most influential of Britain's many clubs and societies. Indeed, it remained so into the twentieth century, if not beyond.

Among the factors that gave Freemasonry widespread appeal was the publication and promulgation of the 1723 Constitutions. The book was pioneering, setting out important Enlightenment principles:

- religious tolerance, something wholly radical in a world characterised by religious conflict;
- meritocracy, at a time when birth and wealth largely determined success;
- high standards of interpersonal civility;
- scientific and artistic education; and
- societal and personal self-improvement.

Freemasonry thus fostered an Enlightenment culture, first nationally and then internationally. And alongside this the 1723 Constitutions can be seen as a fulcrum or pivot on which Freemasonry turned from its medieval past towards a modern present and future.

* * * *

INVENTING THE FUTURE: THE 1723 CONSTITUTIONS

English Freemasonry embraces three 'Grand Principles': 'Brotherly Love', 'Relief' and 'Truth'. But what do these expressions really mean and where do they originate...

Different interpretations have been given over the years but perhaps the most appropriate would be to understand 'Brotherly Love' as a short-hand expression for the practice and promotion of consideration for others, not just brother freemasons but mankind – humanity - taken as a whole. 'Relief' is not simply the provision of charity for the relief of poverty but also the alleviation of 'distress', that is, suffering more generally. And 'Truth' refers principally to education, improving one's knowledge and understanding not just for personal gain but to benefit society more broadly and to understand oneself. There is a direct quote in Masonic ritual that captures this last concept. It states that freemasons are encouraged to focus on the advantages of education, 'by which means alone we are rendered fit members of regularly organized society'.

These ideas are part of a set of principles that lie at the core of modern Freemasonry. They were detailed for the first time in *The Constitutions of the Freemasons* - the '1723 Constitutions' - a book whose Enlightenment tenets provide the philosophical foundations of Freemasonry today.

It has been recognised that the 1723 Constitutions is among Freemasonry's most important documents, and not only in England. In 1730 it was taken by the Grand Lodge of Ireland as the model for the Irish Constitutions and later the basis for *Ahiman Rezon*, the Constitutions of 'Antients' Freemasonry, which in 1813 merged with the Grand Lodge of England to form the United Grand Lodge of England.

The 1723 Constitutions was re-printed verbatim by Benjamin Franklin in 1734 for use in America. It was translated into Dutch (1730), French (1736), and German (1741). And it circulated in its English and foreign language versions throughout Europe in the 1730s and 1740s. Indeed, it set a pattern for Freemasonry throughout the world.

Understanding the context in which the 1723 Constitutions was written helps to explain both the origins of modern Freemasonry and the relationship between Freemasonry and Society today. This book explores that context, as well as examining the content of the 1723 Constitutions and its consequences.

* * * *

John Hamill, the former Librarian at the United Grand Lodge of England, argued in *The Craft*, published in London in 1986, that there was little evidence to support the theory of a gradual shift in Freemasonry from the medieval stonemasons' guilds to the more gentlemanly form of Masonic lodge that emerged in the eighteenth century.

But although Freemasonry's 'traditional history' may have been queried and rejected, Hamill did not put forward an alternative explanation. That omission was one reason his views failed to gain traction and why many freemasons continued (and continue) to cleave to the long-standing and unfounded belief in gradualism, seeking to trace Freemasonry's evolution along a notional thread from time immemorial.

In this book I suggest that despite many aspects of Masonic ritual - 'words and tokens' - that can be dated properly to the medieval period, the Grand Lodge of England and the 1723 Constitutions, and thus modern Freemasonry, emerged in the early decades of the eighteenth century as a consequence of quite different factors.

In this context, modern Freemasonry was not inevitable nor part of a continuing process of measured evolution. It represented a step-change, and one that was taken intentionally.

English Freemasonry altered radically over a short period of little more than a decade from 1717 to mirror the political and philosophical objectives of those who led it. Their mind-set was determined by many factors. These included radical philosophical ideas associated with the European Enlightenment; the threat posed to the newly-crowned George I and his Whig government by the Jacobite supporters of the exiled James Stuart, 'the king over the water', and the fear that he might forcibly seize the British and Irish thrones; and the insecurities stemming from more than a century of religious and political conflict in Britain and Europe.

We can look at each of these in turn.

We spoke earlier about the Enlightenment. The Enlightenment is the name given to a set of philosophical principles that emerged in northern Europe in the late seventeenth and early eighteenth century. Based on the works of John Locke and Isaac Newton, among others, its defining characteristics include a belief in reason, personal liberty, and the search for knowledge through scientific method and rational observation. It was and is a philosophy skeptical of political and religious diktat expressed, for example, by absolute monarchy, hereditary aristocracy, and the unwillingness of established religious (and other) authorities to face questions, a criticism levelled at the Catholic Church in particular.

Enlightenment values embrace religious tolerance, civic responsibility, constitutional government, meritocracy, and the promotion of the societal benefits that flow from courtesy, charity, education and self-improvement. These ideas came to dominate western thought and are embedded in the 1723 Constitutions and in modern Freemasonry.

James Stuart (1688-1766), the exiled Pretender to the British and Irish thrones, and his Jacobite followers, were considered by many to be an existential threat to Hanoverian Britain and to those at its heart: the Whig government and its followers, and those who had supported and benefited from the 'Glorious Revolution' of 1688 and the expulsion of James II and his replacement by William and Mary. (By way of background, the Whigs were a political faction and then a political party that contested political power with the Tories, their political rivals, who were largely excluded from government for half a century.)

The threat from James Stuart and his Jacobite supporters was real, not imagined. As noted before, James's allies included France and Spain, arguably the most powerful countries in Europe, as well as a large minority in Britain who considered the constitutional foundations on which George I, the Elector of Hanover, had been crowned king in 1714 to be legally and morally unsafe. Moreover, George I had made a delicate political situation worse by dismissing the Tories from power the following year, alienating a significant section of the political classes.

The third factor underpinning modern Freemasonry and the development and publication of the 1723 Constitutions was the backdrop of some 150 years of persecution by France of its Protestant – Huguenot – minority, a period of state-sanctioned oppression that verged on genocide.

Some historians have argued that any fear of Protestant harassment that might be instigated by James Stuart in Britain was misplaced and that the Pretender would have favoured religious tolerance and remained in accord with his father's Declaration of Indulgence. But while this is possible and may have afforded a degree of protection, contemporary observers found it difficult to disregard the influence of France and Spain, James Stuart's main supporters, and were acutely aware of - and gave weight - to the persecution by France and Spain of their non-Catholic minorities.

Britain's Whig establishment and the tens of thousands of émigré Huguenots who had found sanctuary in England feared that the consequence of a Jacobite rebellion and Stuart restoration would be the demolition of their political and financial capital. And that it would be accompanied by penal sanction and a wave of persecution.

They had legitimate reasons to be concerned and to understand why we need to track back to 1688.

As we have mentioned, political and religious opposition to the House of Hanover was rooted in the 'Glorious Revolution' that had swept the Catholic James II from the throne to be replaced a year later by the Protestant William III, Prince of Orange and Stadtholder of the Low Countries, and his wife and co-monarch, Mary, James II's eldest daughter.

Whether James II had abdicated or been forced to depart, or in other words had been the subject of a coup, and its corollary, the basis on which William and Mary had been invited by Parliament to succeed as king and queen, was disputed and the way forward unclear. James and William's respective supporters understood the need to debate and resolve the issue – both sides sought political stability - and this took place in the Convention Parliament which met in London in January 1689.

Perhaps surprisingly the discussions were relatively balanced, especially in the House of Lords. James II had hoped to ensure the return of compliant MPs to the Commons from the mid-1680s and in 1689 many in Parliament remained his supporters. He had also moved to broaden his appeal and to reach out to a constituency that included Protestant dissenters and opposition Whigs. But there were parts of the electorate that he found hard to attract, especially where stakeholders had become disaffected by his attempts to force new charters on towns and cities and purge their corporations. And while James II's efforts to widen his circle of support with an offer of religious tolerance may have been genuine, it was trumped by William and Mary who were willing to present not only religious tolerance but also constitutional liberty.

The Convention Parliament's compromise settlement brought together a spectrum of divergent religious and political interests. New constitutional parameters were agreed, a declaration of 'ancient rights' drawn up, and a list proclaimed of those rights deemed to have been violated by James II.

William and Mary were invited to become king and queen of England on 13 February and a parallel Convention of Estates gave them the crown in Scotland. Their coronation took place in London at Westminster Abbey on 11 April and they recognised parliamentary sovereignty openly with an oath to uphold all its laws.

The Declaration of Rights was passed into law as the Bill of Rights and followed in 1701 by the Act of Settlement. This restricted the succession to James I of England's (James VI of Scotland's) Protestant heirs alone. Scotland however declined to pass its own version of the Act, a decision that initiated five years of acrimonious negotiations.

From England's standpoint, the main imperative to bring Scotland into line was to remove the risk that the legal basis for the Protestant succession in England could be challenged by a competing Scottish monarch. This requirement to avoid what might become a potentially mutually destructive contest was the principal driver behind the push for the passage of Acts of Union north and south of the border.

Political union and the loss of parliamentary sovereignty were opposed by many in Scotland. They found voice in the Scottish Act of Security passed in 1704 in which Scotland set down its objections to the same royal succession as in England. London's response was a package of blackmail and bribery.

The Alien Act of 1705 - 'An Act for the Effectual Securing the Kingdom of England from the apparent Dangers that may arise from several Acts lately passed in the parliament of Scotland' -

stated that Scotland must either accept the Hanoverian succession or negotiate to unite the English and Scottish parliaments. If Scotland failed to do so, its principal exports to England, cattle, linen and coal, would be banned and Scots would forfeit their privileges under English law:

> *That from and after the 25 day of December 1705, no Person or Persons being a Native or Natives of the Kingdom of Scotland... shall be capable to inherit any Lands... within this Kingdom of England... or to enjoy any Benefit or Advantage of a natural-born Subject of England: But every such Person shall be from henceforth adjudged and taken as an Alien born out of the allegiance of the Queen of England, until such time as the Succession to the Crown of Scotland, be declared and settled by an Act of Parliament in Scotland.*

At the same time, the elites who dominated the Scottish Parliament were courted with cash and honours. Some £400,000 was distributed, nominally to compensate for the future liabilities that would be assumed in relation to the English national debt but in practice directed at those who had invested in the Company of Scotland's failed Darien Land Scheme in Panama. This had cost its mainly Scottish shareholders around £500,000, a vast sum that had almost bankrupted the country. Other monies were distributed alongside, including £20,000 personally by David Boyle, newly created Earl of Glasgow, one of the commissioners for the Union.

We have already mentioned Burns's comment that Scotland was 'bought and sold for English gold'. It had resonance north of the border and the blatant corruption that accompanied that passage of the Act of Union in the Scottish parliament was heavily resented by many. A decade later it found expression in support for James Stuart and the Jacobite cause.

* * * *

JAMES STUART & THE JACOBITES

The Pretender, James Stuart, tagged 'the king over the water', was the son of the exiled James II and his second wife, Mary of Modena. He was without question Queen Anne's closest relative, her half-brother, but under the Act of Settlement, as a Catholic, had been excluded from the succession and the throne.

Prince George of Hanover, the future George I's claim on the crown was slightly less direct but equally legitimate. The great-grandson of James I and thus James Stuart's second cousin, George's father was Ernst Augustus, Prince Elector of Hanover, and his mother, Sophia of Hanover, the daughter of Elizabeth Stuart, the second child and eldest daughter of James I.

It is a Jacobite myth that there were between thirty and fifty Catholic contenders who had more direct links to Queen Anne than George I. There were six, and all were foreign. But the fable of un-entitlement was assisted by George having been born in Hanover with German as his first language and only limited spoken English.

George I's supporters may have argued - accurately - that his succession was justified by law and hereditary right, but the political reality was that he was crowned as a function of Parliamentary edict: the Act of Settlement. And this was not without opposition both in London and across the country as a whole.

The riots that marked George I's coronation in October 1714 were instigated and supported not only by James Stuart's Jacobite followers but also by many Tories and High Church Anglicans.

The celebratory revelries of Hanoverian loyalists were disrupted by protests in more than twenty towns and cities across England, from Canterbury to Shrewsbury and Taunton to Norwich. Significantly, local Tory magistrates were acquiescent and failed to disperse the 'tumults and riot... universally fomented'. Their inaction was noted and led within days to a parliamentary declaration to suppress the 'Assembly or Rout of People against the Law' and the passage of a Riot Act.

Protests in London were initially restrained. Many leading Tories had given up on a Stuart restoration and self-interestedly recognised George I as king. Indeed, even the Tory Lords Oxford and Bolingbroke were in attendance when the George I's reign was proclaimed formally, with Oxford organising a public bonfire to celebrate the event.

But the concord would be brief. Later the same month defiant protesters obstructed the king's return from the Lord Mayor's banquet and rioting broke out in Whitechapel on the eastern fringe of the City.

Periodic public disturbances continued into 1715 and grew in scope after the parliamentary elections in March in which the Whigs obtained a crushing majority in the House of Commons. A purge of virtually all Tories in central government followed and was repeated on a lesser scale in town and cities, and at county level. This political exodus triggered further anti-Hanoverian riots and demonstrations that swept across England from Bristol and Gloucester to Oxford, Leeds and Manchester.

For George I and his government worse was to come. Taking advantage of the public discontent and building on an existing support base in Scotland, the Earl of Mar raised James Stuart's royal standard at Braemar in September 1715 to foment a rebellion. He met with initial success and a swathe of Scotland went over to the Pretender within the month, as did much of the border country.

Mar's revolt was also emulated on a lesser scale elsewhere, including the Tory-dominated West of England.

London reacted promptly. Troops were despatched to Bristol, Plymouth and Southampton to curtail the insurgents, and intelligence resources exploited to arrest the ringleaders in the West, South West and Wales.

Acts of Attainder were passed against the principal leaders of the opposition, including Lord Bolingbroke. Habeas corpus was suspended. And detachments of the army were hurried north to reinforce the military garrisons in Scotland and protect the North of England and the Midlands.

Hanoverian and Jacobite forces engaged in battles at Sherrifmuir and Inverness, but they were indecisive. They also clashed at Preston in Lancashire, which had fallen to the Jacobites. Loyalist troops surrounded the town and prevailed in November when the arrival of reinforcements forced the Jacobites to agree to an unconditional surrender.

In December 1715 James Stuart finally landed in Perth to stake his claim personally. He was too late. The Jacobite army stood at less than 5,000 men when the Earl of Mar led them the following month. They were defeated and the rebels fell back to Perth, then retreated, demoralised, north-east to Dundee and Montrose. In early February 1716 James Stuart abandoned his supporters and sailed from Scotland to return to exile. He was joined by Mar, Drummond and other prominent Jacobite figureheads. Deserted by its leadership the Jacobite uprising collapsed and its army scattered.

But although the rebellion had failed, the Indemnity Act passed by Parliament in 1717 recognised the need for reconciliation. Many of those captured were pardoned or reprieved, including Lords Carnwath, Widdrington and Nairne. And large numbers of prisoners held at Newgate, Carlisle, Edinburgh and Stirling gaols were freed, as were some 200 rebels captured at Preston. But this was only part of the story. The Jacobite leaders in the Borders and Northumberland, Lords Derwentwater and Kenmure, were found guilty of treason and sentenced to death, and some fifty other rebels suffered the same fate. Alongside, hundreds of James Stuart's supporters were exiled to the American colonies.

However, despite their defeat, the Jacobite threat endured and although described variously as real, imagined, and a contrivance wheeled out by Whig politicians to maintain their political power, the reality was a mix of all three. The hazard may have waxed and waned but protecting Britain and Ireland against another Jacobite Rising coupled to a Spanish or French-backed invasion remained a core tenet of British government policy until the 1750s. Indeed, it was only through luck and good intelligence that two attempted invasions in 1717 and 1719 failed.

Importantly, the danger posed by the Pretender was not exclusively military. There were also powerful philosophical, religious and legal arguments supporting the validity of James Stuart's claim to the throne.

Two rival constitutional arguments competed for dominance in the early eighteenth century. The first, the ascendant view, held that England was governed by a constitution rooted in established custom that could be traced back to Anglo-Saxon times. From this perspective, constitutional governance was the product of a notional balance between the legislature - the King, the Lords and the Commons - and the subjects of the realm, who enjoyed an implicit right to resist autocracy and tyranny. The structure had checks and balances to prevent royal absolutism and examples of popular resistance seeded a narrative that stretched from before Magna Carta to encompass the 'Glorious Revolution'.

John Locke extended this thesis. His *Two Treatises of Government* argued that an absolute monarchy, by definition, made slaves of its subjects and that legitimate government was established by consent and served to secure the rights to life, liberty and property.

In Locke's analysis a government exercised power legitimately only if it did not encroach on the natural rights of the governed. Where such rights had been breached 'the people' had the moral authority to resist and the legal right to dismiss the government and establish a successor:

The great end of men's entering into society being the enjoyment of their properties in peace and safety and the great instrument and means of that being the laws established in that society, the first and fundamental positive law of all commonwealths is the establishing of the legislative power...

To this end it is that men give up all their natural power to the society they enter into and the community put the legislative power into such hands as they think fit with this trust that they shall be governed by declared laws or else their peace, quiet, and property will still be at the same uncertainty as it was in the state of Nature...

The legislative cannot transfer the power of making laws to any other hands, for it being but a delegated power from the people, they who have it cannot pass it over to others. The people alone can appoint the form of the commonwealth which is by constituting the legislative and appointing in whose hands that shall be. And when the people have said 'We will submit and be governed by laws made by such men and in such forms', nobody else can say other men shall make laws for them, nor can they be bound by any laws but such as are enacted by those whom they have chosen and authorised to make laws for them.

Locke's definition of the nature of government was radical and had narrow support in its unvarnished form. It was disavowed by many of those in power who were disinclined to support a theory that could encourage a challenge to their authority. And in the late 1680s it was never intended or asserted that the consent of the public at large was required to approve the transfer of the crown to William and Mary nor that ultimate sovereignty rested with the general population. Both were alien concepts in a society where the franchise was restricted and based on relatively narrowly defined property rights.

This, the mainstream Whig historical perspective on constitutional history, was encapsulated by Edmund Burke towards the end of the eighteenth century when he noted that the 'Glorious Revolution' was to be celebrated precisely *because* it had limited political change to the minimum needed to reinstate the 'ancient constitution'.

Unsurprisingly, a contrarian argument was advanced by James Stuart's supporters. Notwithstanding their tangible political self-interest, the Jacobite's starting point was that there was only one legitimate basis for a constitution: the divine right of kings. From this perspective the authority to govern was derived solely from God and a king ruled his nation by virtue of God's direct command. Hereditary succession was the only means by which a king could and should be replaced and it had thus been unlawful for the Convention Parliament to have interfered with what was an inalienable right.

The unavoidable result of such an analysis was that George I's coronation was neither legally binding nor morally valid.

Such thinking had been a central plank of conventional Catholic teaching for centuries. It was expressed by Dante in *Inferno* where the Ninth Circle of Hell was reserved for those who had committed regicide: the ultimate sin of treachery against God being the slaughter of one whom he had anointed. It was for precisely this reason that Brutus and Cassius were condemned to the Ninth Circle alongside Judas Iscariot.

But support for the Pretender's entitlement to the crown was not restricted to Catholics. The doctrine of hereditary succession was also favoured by non-jurors, those who had refused to swear an oath of allegiance to William and Mary, whose influence belied their relatively modest numbers. Other sections of the Protestant clergy whose support for James Stuart flowed from the oath of loyalty they had sworn to the crown similarly opposed George I.

The issue led to a schism within English and Irish Anglicanism, while in Scotland many highly traditionalist Protestants - Episcopalians - refused to swear allegiance to George I or accept that William and Mary had held office other than as co-regents.

James Stuart had other devotees, especially among those who stood to benefit substantially from his return. And these silos of support were not limited to Tory landowners forced from power by George I and his administration.

France, Spain and Sweden also favoured the Stuart cause for geo-political reasons and successive Whig governments believed rightly that a French or Spanish invasion in tandem with domestic Jacobite insurgence posed a most serious threat to Hanoverian Britain. If successful, the combination would sever the Hanoverian line, dismember the Whig administration, dissipate wealth, and return Britain's political structures to the early 1680s.

Whig concerns were justified and European support for James Stuart was real. Faced with such threats, governments from Lord Stanhope to Sir Robert Walpole maintained a firm anti-Jacobite strategy following the axiom that 'ministerial idleness where Jacobites were concerned was an unaffordable luxury'.

A key component of this policy was the extension of Britain's matrix of formal and informal spy networks. This included the interception and decryption of diplomatic, commercial and private correspondence. Such intelligence was sought by all sides but the required apparatus was arguably most advanced in England.

The seizure of suspect communications centred on the 'Secret Department of the Post Office', with decoding taking place within its Deciphering Branch. Although under the nominal authority of the Postmaster General, the Department was financed by secret service funds and reported to the Secretaries of State.

From 1717 until the 1730s, the government's anti-Jacobite intelligence and surveillance operations fell largely within the remit of Charles Delafaye and Jean Lefevre, two of many Huguenot émigrés given senior and sensitive positions within successive Whig administrations. They were highly trusted not least for their political and philosophical perspective, the consequence of more than a century of religious oppression of the Huguenots by France.

To appreciate this political dynamic it is necessary to go back in time once more, in this case to the first half of the sixteenth century.

HUGUENOT PERSECUTION & EXODUS

The Protestant Reformation began in Germany in the second decade of the sixteenth century and spread rapidly.

Its first French martyr, Jean Vallière, was executed in 1523 and state persecution was stepped-up as Protestantism became synonymous with opposition to the established order, both religious and political.

'L'affaire des placards' in October 1534, a Protestant protest in Paris against the perceived abuses of Roman Catholicism, was accompanied by demonstrations in Blois, Rouen, Tours, Orléans, and other French cities. The authorities responded forcefully with the arrest and execution of twenty-four deemed heretics while others were driven into exile. The latter included John Calvin who fled to Basel and then Geneva, before moving to join Martin Bucer's community of French Protestants in Strasbourg.

Calvin's teachings and his *Institutes of the Christian Religion* encouraged some French émigrés to return home and a small Calvinist community was established at Meauz in the mid-1540s. A church was founded in Paris a decade later and notwithstanding harassment by the Catholic Church, Calvinism expanded.

In 1559, fifteen churches attended a synod in Paris to establish a French Reformed Church. Within a few years the number of affiliated churches exceeded a thousand.

Rapid growth brought the movement into direct conflict with the French Catholic aristocracy and Church hierarchy in France whose power it threatened. And the reaction was violent. The Duke of Guise sanctioned an attack on Calvinist - Huguenot - congregants at Vassy in March 1562, killing over sixty and wounding another hundred. The violence foreshadowed what would develop into more than a century of religious persecution and conflict, something encapsulated by the Saint Bartholomew's Day Massacre in August 1572.

The wedding of Margaret de Valois, the sister of Charles IX, King of France, to Henry de Navarre, a Huguenot prince, was the catalyst for an attempt to assassinate the Protestants' political leaders, not least Gaspard de Coligny, a charismatic aristocrat and decorated admiral.

The plot failed but Charles IX was nonetheless persuaded to permit Coligny's execution and that of other Huguenots following false allegations that they were plotting against him. The move sparked mob violence against the Huguenot community which spread from Paris to cities and towns across France. The word 'massacre' is appropriate. Estimates of the number of Huguenots killed in Paris and over the weeks that followed vary, but the range spans the low tens of thousands to as many as 80,000 or more.

The Catholic hierarchy regarded the carnage as having secured deliverance from heresy, and France from a conspiracy to overturn the state. Pope Gregory XIII sent a congratulatory symbolic golden rose to Charles IX and instructed that a *Te Deum* be sung and a celebratory medal struck. The coin depicts an angel holding a cross and sword standing to the left of a half circle of Huguenot corpses. It is surmounted with the legend *Ugonottorum Strages* - Massacre of the Huguenots. The reverse side carries an image of the Pope.

Protestant countries in Europe were aghast and reports of the massacre by Francis Walsingham, then Elizabeth I's ambassador to France, did much to cement England's pro-Huguenot political stance.

France's Huguenot survivors' attempts to resist further repression were unsuccessful albeit that Henry de Navarre was later crowned Henry IV and promulgated the Edict of Nantes and two royal brevets which offered French Protestants modest protection. However, Henry IV was obliged to convert to Catholicism. Around 85% of the French population was Catholic and Henry required the support of the Catholic Church to govern.

Henry IV was assassinated in 1610 (he was deemed a usurper by some extremist Catholics and there were around a dozen attempts on his life), and the persecution of the Huguenots resumed under his son, Louis XIII. One example is the siege of La Rochelle, a Huguenot enclave, in 1628, during which La Rochelle's population plummeted from 27,000 to 5,000 through starvation and disease. It led to an unconditional surrender.

Although the Huguenots were no longer a political threat, the French state maintained an anti-Huguenot stance and harassment continued. Some three-quarters of France's 800 Protestant churches were razed in the three decades to 1685, and thousands of Huguenots forcibly converted to Catholicism. Those who refused faced 'insupportable violence', the destruction or confiscation of their estates, and imprisonment or death.

Under Louis XIV, Huguenot mistreatment reached an apogee in the 1680s with the *Dragonnades*, the billeting of French dragoons on Huguenot households, a policy that became synonymous with violence, rape and theft.

And compounding the Huguenots' difficulties, Louis XIV rescinded the Edict of Nantes in 1685. The limited protections that had applied under its aegis were removed, effectively depriving French Protestants of their remaining civil and religious liberties.

Huguenot migration from France accelerated in response. What had been a trickle of refugees from the mid-sixteenth century became a torrent. Despite the penal risks, almost a third of France's Huguenot population escaped, an estimated 250,000 people, with more leaving in later years.

Many migrated to the Low Countries, the United Provinces. Others settled in the German states and Switzerland. A small number migrated to North America and Southern Africa. But the most popular destination was England, with more than 50,000 refugees, the majority settling in London. There they joined an existing community which was itself the product of Huguenot flight over the preceding century.

The influx had a substantial impact with the incoming refugees representing around 10% of London's 500,000 population. The British establishment was sympathetic however and sought to ensure that their co-religionists received tangible support. Contributions were made from the Civil List, with William and Mary donating almost £40,000 between 1689-93, with additional monies given by the aristocracy and Parliament. Charitable donations were also provided via parish collections. In total more than £100,000 was raised, with additional contributions from the Royal Bounty Fund made into the eighteenth century.

The Huguenot community in London had conformist and non-conformist branches but both shared an allegiance to their new home and to the English crown. This was especially evident in the military where hundreds of Huguenot officers joined William and Mary's army. Their number included Henri de Massue, whose success at the Battle of Aughrim in 1691 led to his promotion to commander-in-chief in Ireland and his subsequent elevation to the Irish peerage as Viscount Galway. In 1694 as a lieutenant general he commanded an English force alongside the Duke of Savoy against France. He was created Earl of Galway in 1697.

Five Huguenot regiments were established by William III, with three Huguenot battalions of Foot raised in 1689. Other professional officers were supernumeraries, attached to regiments of Horse or Foot and serving on half pay until vacancies became available. In doing so they provided a reservoir of potential officers, 'proven and trustworthy'. Indeed, it has been estimated that up to a fifth of England's army officers were Huguenots, around 1,000 in total. But the number may have been even higher given that some 3,000 officers left Louis XIV's service after the Revocation.

Although the 1713 Treaty of Utrecht brought three decades of relative peace between Britain and France, Huguenot persecution persisted and recognition of the Protestant faith in France continued to be denied. And barely two years later, England's Huguenot émigrés faced danger once again: 'l'invasion d'un prétendant papist', the 1715 Jacobite Rising.

The prospect of a Catholic monarch on the British throne was regarded as an existential threat by Huguenots and Whigs alike. It would remain so for more than three decades as the 1715 Rising was followed by another attempted invasion of Britain (backed by Spain) in 1717, yet another in 1719, and by the Atterbury Plot in 1721-2. Other alarms would follow, culminating in a second Jacobite Rising in 1745.

This insecurity was at the root of the widespread belief among Huguenots and Whigs that the institutions which shielded them and maintained the Hanoverian status quo required if not demanded their support.

The same pattern was etched onto Freemasonry with the Grand Lodge of England reconfiguring the Charges and Regulations and parts of Masonic ritual to promote and advance an Enlightenment agenda.

Although the book is often called 'Anderson's Constitutions', after James Anderson who wrote the traditional history and other text, the Charges were written by Jean Theophilus Desaguliers and the Regulations written and compiled by his friend and colleague, George Payne. Taken together, they promote an Enlightenment philosophy, facilitate Masonic governance, and advance a pro-government and pro-Hanoverian agenda. They are the principal elements of the 1723 Constitutions and are discussed in detail later in this book.

Lodge ritual and Masonic practices were reconfigured at the same time with meetings flavoured with Enlightenment ideas and lectures that explained and explored the arts and sciences. These sentiments were incorporated prominently into Bernard Creake's

1731 pirated edition of the Constitutions which quoted Edward Oakley, a founder of the Nag's Head Lodge in Carmarthen and Master of the Three Compasses Lodge in Silver Street, London:

> *Those of the Brotherhood whose Genius is not adapted to Building, I hope will be industrious to improve in, or at least to love, and encourage some Part of the seven Liberal Sciences... it is necessary for the Improvement of Members of a Lodge, that such Instruments and Books be provided, as be convenient and useful in the exercise, and for the Advancement of this Divine Science of Masonry, and that proper Lectures be constantly read in such of the Sciences, as shall be thought to be most agreeable to the Society, and to the honour and Instruction of the Craft.*

These were not the only changes. Freemasonry continued to evolve and in the second half of the eighteenth century was influenced greatly by the London Irish and the 'Grand Lodge of England according to the Old Institutions': the 'Antients Grand Lodge'.

Antients Freemasonry became, in part, a proto friendly society providing mutual support and a discrete social space for the growing number of aspirational middling and lower middling who sought to join Freemasonry in Britain, America, and elsewhere. But this would be a half-century later. In the early 1720s the Masonic circle at the helm of the Grand Lodge of London & Westminster (later renamed the Grand Lodge of England) was more elitist, intentionally positioning the organisation to capture the heights of English society.

The construct that emerged was materially different from that which preceded it and as a result Freemasonry became within two short decades the most prominent and influential of Britain's many fraternal clubs and associations.

And Freemasonry was not limited to London. Within a few years it boasted a uniquely large provincial network and a presence overseas where its expansion was bound to migration, the military, political influence, and international, especially colonial, trade.

Grand Lodge's leadership also associated Freemasonry with science, with a world that could be measured, analysed and explained. And they linked it with antiquarianism and the growing desire to understand and explore the past.

Alongside and equally appealing to its members and potential members were Freemasonry's connections with and support from celebrated members of the aristocracy, its seeming exclusivity, and its well-publicised role as a space offering clubbable fraternal association.

A contemporary rhyme described this aspect succinctly, if somewhat ironically:

We make for Five guineas, the price is but small,
And then Lords and Dukes, you your Brothers may call,
Have gloves, a White Apron, get drunk and that's all. [1]

English Freemasonry in the 1720s and 1730s captured the contemporary zeitgeist. And its success was such that copies emerged rapidly elsewhere. Grand Lodges were established in Ireland (1725) and Scotland (1736), Provincial Grand Lodges and Lodges formed across America, and Grand Lodges and Lodges were established throughout continental Europe, including France, the Netherlands, Sweden, Austria, Germany, and Russia.

In parts of continental Europe Freemasonry's presence within the aristocracy and the military, and its popularity among intellectuals and politicians, gave rise to concerns, especially among the senior ranks of the establishment and Church who believed it to be a threat.

---

[1] A Gentleman, *Love's last shift: or, the mason disappointed...* (London, *c.*1720).

One consequence was the 1738 bull issued by Pope Clement XII denouncing Freemasonry. The bull noted that Freemasonry was inter-denominational, composed of 'men of any religion or sect, satisfied with the appearance of natural probity, [and] joined together, according to their laws and the statutes laid down for them, by a strict and unbreakable bond'.[2] However, Freemasonry was nonetheless considered a threat to 'the peace of the temporal state' and a challenge to the authority of church doctrine. Over time it would be countered by the threat of excommunication and in Spain, Italy, Portugal and elsewhere, by prohibition, restriction, and the Inquisition.

Other objections were raised on the grounds of a menace to national security. Private discussions in societies where debate was circumscribed were not tolerated easily and the argument was advanced that 'if they [freemasons] were not doing evil they would not have so great a hatred of the light'.

But despite such opposition, Freemasonry grew in popularity to the extent that the Lodge came to be positioned close to the heart of eighteenth-century polite society. And not just in England, Wales, Ireland and Scotland, but also in America, across Britain's growing Empire, and throughout many countries in continental Europe, from where it spread to Latin America and elsewhere.

The development was momentous and to gain a sense of historical perspective it is helpful to go back 300 years to medieval England and to the Black Death.

* * * *

[2] *In Eminenti*, Papal Bull of Pope Clement XII, 28 April 1738.

FREEMASONRY'S ORIGINS

Some commentators have argued that the pursuit of a single point of origin for English Freemasonry should be regarded as an unproductive dead end. Nonetheless, if one were to search for such a point it would be hard to ignore the tectonic shifts in the economic and social fabric that accompanied and followed the Black Death (1348-49) in which some 40% or more of England's population died.

The soaring mortality from the outbreak of Europe's worst plague pandemic led to widespread labour shortages and market dislocations which triggered a sharp rise in wage rates.

In England, Parliament reacted by passing legislation to suppress the cost of labour.

Approved in 1349, Edward III's *Ordinance of Labourers* was designed to cut labourers' pay to the levels that had applied in 1346 before the Black Death had wreaked its havoc. The *Statute of Labourers* enacted in 1351 reinforced the regulations by imposing piecework and daily wage rates for specific occupations. And other laws followed.

The obligation to enforce such laws was incorporated by statute into the duties of the magistracy and by the end of the fourteenth century local justices of the peace were empowered to determine at their discretion what they deemed 'reasonable' wage rates for their districts. Other regulations restricted labour mobility and skewed the terms of contracts in favour of employers.

England's landowner-dominated Parliament had a clear vested interest in seeking to ensure that low-cost labour was available for their estates. Such landowners, the gentry, and others from their circles also served as local magistrates with responsibility for enforcing the law.

The conflict between the landed interest and agricultural and artisanal labour was clear. And it persisted in the wake of further outbreaks of plague throughout the latter half of the century. It resulted in what is probably the best-known example of resistance to parliamentary diktat: the Peasants' Revolt of 1381, a movement catalysed by Parliament's imposition of higher taxes.

But despite believing the contrary, England's government was unable to legislate away the economic reality of demand and supply. Faced with labour shortages, the nominal cash wages of skilled building workers in southern England rose by two-thirds over the second half of the fourteenth century, from 3d per day in the mid-1340s to 5d per day in the 1390s and that of unskilled labourers doubled to around 3d per day. Indeed, adjusted for inflation, real wages are estimated to have risen by between 50-60%.

Nonetheless, the position soon altered. Knoop and Jones in *The Medieval Mason* draw a graphic portrait of how this unfolded as real wage increases reversed and then declined across much of England during the fifteenth, sixteenth, and seventeenth centuries as prices rose six-fold and workers' pay failed to maintain parity.

The principal trigger for what became more than two centuries of sustained price inflation was an unprecedented expansion in money supply. It was linked to the inflow of New World bullion, large-scale silver mining in central Europe, and the debasement of coinage by English monarchs.

But notwithstanding falling real wages, labour markets remained subject to hostile legislation and local pay negotiations menaced by judicial intervention.

The decline in real earnings for stonemasons and other workers – skilled and unskilled – set the context for the transformation of what had previously been predominantly religious guilds into operative guilds. It also saw the advent of pay rates established through local collective bargaining. Both were visible parts of a process through which craftsmen began to combine for their mutual economic benefit and protection.

These changes are reflected in the scope and content of the 'Old Charges', the first written evidence of early English Freemasonry. The *Regius* and *Cooke* manuscripts, two of the earliest Old Charges dating from the 1390s and 1450s, mention pay specifically, arguing hard that employers should pay wages that take into account and accommodate inflation:

> *pay thy felows after the coste as vytaylys goth thenne... and pay them trwly, apon thy fay, what that they deserve.*

> In translation: *pay your workers in line with the cost of food; truly, pay them what they deserve*

It was from this period that artisans, including stonemasons, carpenters and other trades created what became 'closed shops' to establish and preserve local monopolies to control labour supply, thereby influencing wage rates. Guilds justified restrictive practices with arguments that included improving training, enhancing quality control, and enforcing contracts more effectively.

Membership of a guild – effectively the supply of labour – was limited by restricting the number of apprenticeships, enforcing a minimum period for training, and managing the progression of those within the guild.

In broad terms, the guilds' activities were designed to raise or support the price of their members' wages and to protect what were regarded as proprietary skills from untrained 'cowans', those outsiders who had not served an approved apprenticeship. Although the guilds also provided rudimentary mutual financial assistance and basic general education, this was secondary to their main purpose: to protect their members' income and privileges. The development has been termed 'syndicalist', and it is hard not to concur.

Having been admitted to a stonemasons' guild, a member would progress through three stages from initiation, that is, acceptance into the guild as an apprentice, through to the intermediate position of 'craftsman' or 'journeyman' mason. And finally, at completion of the apprenticeship, a journeyman would be accorded the status of a fully trained 'master mason'.

At initiation and at each stage of the progression from apprentice to fellowcraft, and fellowcraft to master mason, the candidate would swear an oath to keep secret the guild's operational methodology. In return he would be entrusted with the 'working secrets' of each rank and be given a password, sign, and token.

Training would last for at least seven years. The minimum age at entry was fourteen and that to be raised to a master mason was twenty-one, the legal age of maturity.

The pace at which a candidate progressed was a function of skill, tradition and economic conditions. There was no point in allowing an apprentice to advance if insufficient work was available; and conversely, a financial advantage accrued to a master mason, in effect a small business owner, via exploitation of their apprentices and fellowcraft, legally indentured labour, during years of high demand.

Stonemasons' skills were fundamental to the construction of the cathedrals, churches, town halls and city walls that commanded the religious and secular heights of medieval society. And unlike many other craftsmen and agricultural labourers, skilled masons had qualified flexibility to travel to work on different construction sites.

It has been argued that such relative autonomy is the explanation of the term 'freemason'. There are, however, alternative and more robust explanations. One is that the word derives from a shortened form of 'Freestone Mason', referring to a stonemason qualified to work with freestone, the best form of stone and one capable of being worked without shattering.

Since freestone was relatively expensive, a mason would usually be fully trained before being permitted to work it. Such skilled masons were thus called 'free' masons to distinguish them from 'rough' or ordinary masons.

Others reach a similar conclusion, albeit via a different route, arguing that 'free' was derived linguistically from 'noble' or 'superior', and that the term was used to denote a skilled worker able to command a premium rate of pay over and above a 'rough' or less expert mason.

Contemporary records hold numerous examples of the term being used in this way. One example is from a petition supporting a Richard Hardwick of Shepton Mallet who had been indicted for working as a 'free mason' when qualified only as a 'rough mason'.

Over the course of the sixteenth and seventeenth centuries the guilds' social and financial influence increased as they became integrated into and embedded within local civic political structures, especially in London and England's larger provincial cities such as Chester and York.

Alongside their local political influence, which included the right to nominate members to the city council, other social and financial connections linked the guilds to the municipal authorities, and *vice versa*. At the same time, guild membership shifted over time to become increasingly dominated by master builders and business owners.

Such men had a similar standing to other civic burghers and broadly comparable financial interests. In this context it has been argued, probably correctly, that local merchant and artisan oligarchies controlled England's towns and cities and manipulated the guild system to advance their self-interests. Indeed, the prevailing conditions of relatively inefficient and parochial markets facilitated such exploitation:

> *Monopoly was of the essence of economic life in this epoch... since the municipal authority had the right to make regulations as to who*

should trade and when they should trade; it possessed a considerable power of turning the balance of trade in [its own] favour.

Self-interest also encouraged the guilds (or lodges) to admit local dignitaries to their ranks. The advantages were tangible, especially since local magistrates continued to hold the authority to settle wage claims based on local market conditions, a practice reaffirmed in the sixteenth century with the passage of the *Statute of Artificers.*

Local politicians - aldermen, sheriffs and mayors - were also responsible for commissioning civic building works and granting guild charters. And the higher membership fees that could be charged to such non-working members offered a useful source of additional income, providing a financial subsidy to the guild.

This functionalist interpretation has been advanced by Marxist and Masonic historians alike. Referring to 'a very old manuscript', William Preston, after whom the annual Prestonian Lectures are named, noted at the end of the eighteenth century that

When the Master and Wardens met in a lodge, if need be, the sheriff of the county, or the mayor of the city, or alderman of the town, in which the congregation is held, should be made fellow and sociate to the Master, in help of him against rebels.

Municipalities received fees, taxes, and a share in the fines levied by the guilds, and by admitting non-working members the guilds cemented their relationships with their clients and influence over wage rates. The status quo endured until the late seventeenth century when changes to working practices combined with disquiet at the guilds' conservatism and opposition to innovation and free trade, led them to be cast as a brake on commercial progress and to the curtail of their authority.

* * * *

THE OLD CHARGES

Throughout the seventeenth century the masons' guilds, like other guilds, retained elements of medieval ritual, including passwords, signs and codes of conduct, alongside a traditional history written not as accurate record but to secure give legitimacy by dating the origins of masonry to a distant past.

The *Cooke* MS asserted that masonry was introduced 'seven generations' after Adam:

> *before Noah's flood, there was a man that was named Lamech... he begat two sons... the elder son ... was the first man that ever found geometry and Masonry.* [Cooke MS, lines 160-80.]

And where the *Regius* MS and other early manuscripts dated the arrival of masonry in England to King Athelstan, an iconic Anglo-Saxon king reigning in the early tenth century, the *Cooke* MS pushed the date back even further to the third century and St Alban, the earliest English Christian martyr, noting that 'Saint Alban loved well masons, and he gave them... their charges and manners first in England'.

It is notable that the *Cooke* MS states that contemporary wage rates had been 'approved' by Athelstan, who had also endowed his royal imprimatur to masonic guilds and assemblies:

> *and he loved well masonry and masons. And he became a mason himself, and he gave them charges and names as it is now used in England, and in other countries. And he ordained that they should have reasonable pay and purchased a free patent of the king that they should make [an] assembly when they saw a reasonable time.* [Cooke MS, lines 625-37.]

And it was similarly not a coincidence that Old Charges written in York in the mid-sixteenth century echoed the then current labour discontent: the wages demanded by striking workers in 1552 were identical to those set out in the 'traditional history' that referred to pay rates supposedly in place centuries earlier - '2*s* 6*d* a week for work and 3*d* a day for food'.

The Old Charges reflected their contemporary context. References to St Athelstan and St Alban supplied a framework in which technically unlawful wage bargaining was justified by the precedent of history and tradition.

Nonetheless, as the membership of guilds altered during the seventeenth century to become less operative in nature, the Old Charges became less important for their substance than their form.

The admission of gentlemen to guilds or lodges has been advanced as evidence of the beginning of spiritual or speculative Freemasonry. But although such gentlemen may have been driven in part by a desire to experience esoteric traditions, many, and probably most, had different motives.

A minority would have acted as benefactors, attending the Lodge rarely and in a parallel capacity to the patron of a religious order. But for most gentlemen, Lodge membership was a matter of networking accompanied by fraternal socialising.

Medieval historians have commented that feasting and drinking were in the Middle Ages regarded as the defining activities of the guilds: 'if it were not for the feasting, few or none would come'. They also note the ritualistic and charitable aspects of formal dining and its function in the fifteenth and sixteenth centuries as a means whereby 'links of solidarity and patronage could be forged'.

There is little reason to believe that the position was different in the seventeenth century and that gentlemen joined a lodge for reasons that had little to do with spirituality other than in the sense that almost everything through to the seventeenth century was deemed to have a spiritual component.

Many Lodges, including those in Warrington, Chester and York, evolved to the point where almost all members were gentlemen, and that over time they perpetuated their influence through invitations to friends and successive generations of family such that the Lodge became a *de facto* fraternal society.

This point was recognised by the Masonic historian Neville Barker Cryer. Reflecting on the status of Chester Masonry in the seventeenth century, Barker Cryer noted that by the 1660s the Lodge was 'made up largely of the city fathers'. Indeed, Lewis and Thacker's *History of the County of Chester* makes a similar point.

Barker Cryer's commentary on Freemasonry in Yorkshire in the early 1700s also supports the argument. York's membership included many of the city's first families, with masonry having the 'support and patronage of significant Yorkshire gentry'. In Barker Cryer's words, by the beginning of the eighteenth century, Yorkshire masonry had carved a 'notable niche for itself socially'.

The same applies to Staffordshire masonry, reports of which were penned by Elias Ashmole, John Aubrey and Robert Plot, each of whom underscored the presence of gentlemen masons. Although their work has been put forward as evidence of a 'spiritual' form of masonry, their description as 'freemasons' as opposed to 'masons' does not suggest that masonry was in transition.

It demonstrates simply that several gentlemen were present, something that had been common for more than a century.

* * * *

LONDON FREEMASONRY

Given the subsequent importance of London and the Grand Lodge of England, it might be regarded as ironic that in the first decade of the eighteenth century, Freemasonry had only a relatively limited presence in London and the South of England. As James Anderson notes in the 1738 edition of the Constitutions, 'in the South the Lodges were more and more disused... and the annual Assembly... not duly attended'.

Anderson did however qualify his comments slightly, stating that although 'particular lodges were not so frequent and mostly occasional in the South', there were exceptions, with lodges 'in or near the Places where great Works were carried on'.

This was almost certainly an embroidery. There is no evidence to indicate the presence of gentlemanly lodges 'at St Thomas's Hospital', 'in Piccadilly over against St James's Church', 'near Westminster Abbey', 'near Covent Garden', 'in Holborn', or 'on Tower-Hill'. And despite Anderson's comments to the contrary, there is nothing to suggest that William III was privately made a Mason nor that he 'assented' to the choice of Christopher Wren as Grand Master.

But although Anderson may have exaggerated their number and nature, there *is* evidence that Masonic Lodges existed in London and southern England in the early eighteenth century. In addition to the four lodges that founded the new Grand Lodge in 1717 and others that subsequently joined its orbit, we can point to the 1st Duke of Richmond's lodge at Chichester.

So, we can now move to the next section of this book and examine the content and creators of the 1723 Constitutions.

* * * *

List of Regular Lodges as Constituted 'till March 25th 1725
Engraved by John Pine (1690-1756)
Frontispiece by Sir James Thornhill (c.1675-1734)

THE GRAND LODGE OF ENGLAND

The Grand Lodge of England was in large part the creation of an inner circle, many of whose members were part of the 2nd Duke of Richmond's Lodge in Westminster. This had met at the Rummer & Grapes Tavern in Channel Row before moving in the early 1720s to the Horn Tavern in nearby New Palace Yard.

The Lodge's members included aristocrats, politicians, public officials and scientists, and, perhaps most significantly, the Rev. Dr Jean Theophilus Desaguliers.

JEAN THEOPHILUS DESAGULIERS

Arguably the principal driving force behind the formation of the Grand Lodge of London & Westminster and the publication of the 1723 Constitutions, Desaguliers was a Huguenot émigré who had fled France as a child and been brought up in London. He was bright and diligent, and rose from poverty to matriculate and graduate from Oxford University, from where he later obtained a doctorate, and achieved status as a Fellow of the Royal Society and one of the country's leading consulting engineers and scientific educators.

He became a popular and well-paid public lecturer, described by his lead patron, the Duke of Chandos, as 'the best mechanic in Europe', and by a twentieth-century historian as 'arguably the most successful scientific lecturer of the century'.

Under Desaguliers' aegis and with the support of influential friends and colleagues, including several within the Horn Tavern Lodge, the largest and most influential of London's lodges, English Freemasonry was transformed into an organisation that both reflected and reinforced the philosophical and political transformation underway in Britain.

Rev. Dr Jean Theophilus Desaguliers
T.R. Beaufort Hinks (1901)
after a 1725 mezzotint by Peter Pelham (c.1695-1753)

Within a few years of its inception, the new Grand Lodge of England adopted radical Enlightenment principles that included religious tolerance and the promotion of meritocracy and constitutional government.

Desaguliers' associates included George Payne; Martin Folkes, later President of the Royal Society; Alexander Chocke, a Westminster magistrate and a senior figure at the Exchequer, Deputy Grand Master in 1727; William Cowper, Clerk to the Parliaments and chair of the magistrates bench, the first Secretary to Grand Lodge and subsequently DGM; Nathaniel Blackerby, another senior magistrate, an office holder at the Exchequer, another DGM (1728 & 1729) and the first Grand Treasurer (1731); and the Hon. George Carpenter, later 2nd Baron Carpenter of Killaghy, MP for Morpeth, and GW (1729). And we can add to these the publishers, John Senex and John Hooke, and the engraver, John Pine.

Desaguliers was born on 12 March 1683 at Aytré, a village near La Rochelle, to a Huguenot family that fled France for England via Guernsey the same year. Brought up in relative poverty, his father was one of several poorly paid deacons at the Swallow Street church near Piccadilly, Desaguliers was educated by his father who later established a school in Islington, then a village north of the City of London, and then at Bishop Vesey's School in Sutton Coldfield.

In 1705, Desaguliers was admitted to Christ Church, Oxford, as a servitor scholar, reading divinity and being taught experimental natural philosophy by John Keill (1671-1721), a member of the Council of the Royal Society and an acolyte of Sir Isaac Newton, its then President.

Keill introduced Desaguliers to Newton and to the Duke of Chandos, one of England's wealthiest men and a fellow member of the Royal Society's Council. Both men boosted Desaguliers' career. Newton's sponsorship led to his election as a Fellow, with Desaguliers' entrance and ongoing fees waived 'in consideration of his great usefulness to the Royal Society'. And in Chandos Desaguliers secured a well-connected and entrepreneurial patron.

Desaguliers obtained his BA in 1709 and was ordained a deacon in the Church of England the following year by Bishop Compton at Fulham Palace. He received his MA in 1712 and in 1713, following his marriage to Joanna Pudsey, settled in London. He returned to Oxford periodically to lecture and was awarded a doctorate in 1719.

In London Desaguliers lived first in Plough Yard close to the Royal Society's premises in Crane Court. But in 1715 he moved to Channel Row, Westminster. He remained there until 1735 when the area was razed to clear the approach to the new Westminster Bridge. Desaguliers' house was close to the Rummer & Grapes tavern and to New Palace Yard, home to George Payne and many of Desaguliers' other colleagues at Grand Lodge. New Palace Yard was also the location of the Horn Tavern, where the Duke of Richmond's Lodge at the Rummer & Grapes later relocated, probably because it offered more spacious accommodation.

Alongside his lectures and demonstrations at the Royal Society, Desaguliers also lectured publicly. Scientific lectures had become fashionable. Science was emerging into popular culture and interest in Newton's theories had spread beyond Oxbridge and the Royal Society to coffee houses and taverns. Desaguliers' experiments and lectures entertained as well as informed as he displayed and explained to his audiences the effects of electricity, the physical properties of gases, the power of hydraulics, the wonders of optics, and the orbits of the moon and planets.

Within a few years Desaguliers had become the pre-eminent Newtonian lecturer on the private and public lecture circuits. He understood clearly that the commercialisation of science, especially engineering, could address practical concerns and supply workable solutions.

Science was becoming less theoretical and more empirical and in Stephen Pumfrey's words had been 'infiltrated by the values of trade, the marketplace and the monied interest'. And as this trend progressed, Desaguliers became more involved in practical problem solving, from pumping water out of mine workings to pumping drinking water from rivers to towns and cities.

Desaguliers was probably introduced to Freemasonry by George Payne, Richmond's Deputy Master at the Horn. And in addition to the Horn, Desaguliers became a member of other London Lodges, including Solomon's Temple and the Bear & Harrow.

As one of the most senior and well-regarded members of the Grand Lodge of England, its Grand Master in 1719, Deputy Grand Master thrice thereafter, and Master of several important constituent lodges, Desaguliers was a pivotal figure. He was instrumental in re-working the Charges and transforming English Ritual, including the introduction of a third – Master Masons' - degree in around 1723. Prior to this there were only two degree ceremonies: Entered Apprentice and Fellowcraft.

Desaguliers also helped develop a federal governance structure for Freemasonry, oversaw the introduction of lectures at lodge meetings, developed the concept of a Grand Steward and a Grand Stewards' Lodge, and introduced (or 'revived' as he put it) the 'ancient toasts' at lodge dinners. He also promoted Masonic sociability and benevolence and played a key part in maintaining Freemasonry's public image and promoting its principles.

* * * *

GEORGE PAYNE

George Payne (c.1685-1757), was born in Chester to Samuel Payne and Frances Kendrick. The family's assets had once been relatively substantial, 'barns, stables, yards, meadows and pasture', but may have declined in value, a status suggested by the legal actions taken against his father in 1703-4 for debt and damages. George Payne did not attend Oxford or Cambridge, but his younger brother, Thomas (1689-1744), matriculated at Christ Church, Oxford, as a servitor scholar, studying theology alongside Desaguliers. After graduation, Thomas was engaged as chaplain at New College. He was subsequently appointed Canon of Windsor, a chaplain to the king, and a prebendary of Wells Cathedral.

George Payne moved from Chester to London in around 1711 to become a clerk in the Leather Office in St Martin's Lane, a job he would have obtained through family connections. Payne's name and office address feature in classified advertisements for Desaguliers' lectures, being one of several locations where tickets and copies of Desaguliers' 'catalogue of experiments' could be purchased. The date of the advertisements - 1713 – confirms that Payne was known to Desaguliers before Desaguliers had moved to London. And the probability is that Thomas Payne had introduced Desaguliers to his older brother while at Oxford.

Payne was employed in various divisions of the Taxes Office and enjoyed steady promotion over some forty years, principally via seniority. In 1713 he was one of two assistants to the Accomptant General, earning £50 per annum. In 1716 he was promoted to become the senior of two principal clerks at the Taxes Office with an annual salary of £60. And two years later Payne was promoted again, becoming First Clerk and Assistant where he worked directly for Francis Sorrel, whose subordinate he would remain for the next twenty-five years.

Thurſday Morning died, at his Houſe in New Palace-Yard, Weſtminſter, Francis Sorrel, Eſq; one of his Majeſty's Juſtices of the Peace for the City and Liberty of Weſtminſter, and Secretary to the Hon. the Commiſſioners of the Land-Tax, which Place he enjoy'd upwards of thirty Years. And

George Payne, Eſq; Deputy Secretary in that Office, was the ſame Day appointed by the Lords of the Treaſury to ſucceed him; Mr. Hamerſly ſucceeds George Payne, Eſq; as Deputy Secretary; Mr. Antwiſle ſucceeds Mr. Hamerſly in his Office; and Mr. Lee ſucceeds Mr. Antwiſle.

Payne's salary is recorded in *Magnae Britanniae* as being £80 per annum, but this was supplemented by various sinecures, including 'carrying Treasury warrants for taking the Receiver General's securities to the King's Remembrancer's Office'. Treasury Papers mention him in the 1730-40s, noting that he succeeded Sorrel as Secretary to the Tax Commissioners in 1743 at an annual salary of £90, 'plus the usual perquisites'.

Payne's sinecures included appointment as a commissioner for the construction of Westminster Bridge, a project with which several other freemasons were involved; a manager for the Westminster Bridge lottery; and a Lottery Commissioner. All were potentially profitable positions. By the late 1740s, he had sufficient social status to be mentioned in the gossip columns in 1748 and 1749 in connection with the marriage of his nieces: Frances, to the Hon. George Compton; and Catherine, to the Very Rev. Lord Francis Seymour, fifth son of the 8th Duke of Somerset.

Payne was now deemed a gentleman and was described as such in the Westminster polling lists. He had been accorded the title of 'esquire' within Grand Lodge since 1725.

Payne was also one of many magistrates among the ranks of London freemasons. It was no coincidence. Magistrates occupied a pivotal position in eighteenth-century England and nowhere was this more the case than in London. It is thus unsurprising that up to a third of justices on the Middlesex and Westminster benches were freemasons: a pro-government stance united both.

Payne served as the second and fourth Grand Master of Grand Lodge in 1718 and 1720, and was subsequently Senior Grand Warden (1724) and Deputy Grand Master (1735). He appears in the 1723 Constitutions as the Master of the Horn Tavern Lodge, deputising for the Duke of Richmond, and in 1749 was Master of the influential King's Arms Lodge in the Strand. But this skims the surface of a Masonic career that was as active and important as that of Desaguliers.

Payne's commitment to Freemasonry is evident throughout his Masonic career, and not only in his willingness to compile the General Regulations and devote time on behalf of Grand Lodge. His activities are documented in Grand Lodge minutes from the 1720s through to the 1750s and suggest that Payne was regarded highly: appointed to the key Charity Committee in 1727; acting Grand Master in 1735 in Viscount Weymouth's absence; and appointed to the committees advising on the Calcutta Lodge (1741) and the revision of the Constitutions (1754).

Despite his seniority Payne maintained a relatively low public profile and his life is largely unrecorded. He received a few brief mentions in *Ars Quatuor Coronatorum (AQC)*, the Transactions of Quatuor Coronati Lodge, the premier lodge of Masonic research, but there is limited biographical data and other sources contain even less.

This lack of information has led to Payne being considered subordinate to Desaguliers and an adjunct to James Anderson, whose reputation was elevated as a result. But a study of government and parliamentary papers and of Payne's personal and professional networks suggests that such an interpretation would be wrong.

* * * *

JAMES ANDERSON

James Anderson (c.1679-1739), is almost indelibly attached to the 1723 Constitutions. Born and educated in Aberdeen, Anderson was ordained into the Church of Scotland in 1707 and afterwards moved to London to take up a ministry at the Glass House Street congregation before transferring to the Presbyterian church in Swallow Street in 1710. From 1734-39 he ministered at the Lisle Street Chapel.

Anderson is regarded as pivotal to the birth of Modern Freemasonry but he was not the fulcrum on which Grand Lodge and Modern Freemasonry turned. He lacked the social, scientific and political networks of Desaguliers, Payne, and others such as Martin Folkes, William Cowper and Charles Delafaye. Nor did Anderson have the required connections to the aristocracy and upper middling. Indeed, his close identification with the 1723 Constitutions is ironic given that he was not the principal author nor the instigator of the work, albeit that he was responsible for the 1738 edition of the Constitutions.

David Stevenson's analysis of Anderson and his influence on eighteenth-century English Freemasonry is based on Anderson's own account of events set out in the 1738 Constitutions. Although there are other records, the 1738 Constitutions is a principal source for the creation of the Grand Lodge of England, the selection of its early Grand Masters, and the adoption of the Charges and Regulations.

Stevenson argues that Anderson's importance lies in his authorship of the first two official editions of the Constitutions, the provision of a Masonic history that emphasised the Craft's antiquity and his record of Grand Lodge's development. Stevenson's views are shared by other historians who emphasise Anderson's close relationship with Desaguliers, both of whom were members of the Horn Tavern and Solomon's Temple.

However an alternative and counter argument holds that the most significant components of the 1723 Constitutions – the Charges and Regulations – were produced not by Anderson but by Desaguliers and Payne, and that Anderson was engaged in effect as a hired pen and worked under the direction of Desaguliers and the publishers, John Senex and John Hooke.

The preamble to the 1723 Constitutions supports this view. The Dedication to the Duke of Montagu is written by Desaguliers, not Anderson, who comments that he, Desaguliers, is dedicating the book to the past Grand Master – '*I* humbly dedicate' – and not doing so on behalf of others.

Within the Dedication Desaguliers refers to 'the author' as having 'compared and made everything agreeable to History and Chronology'. The absence of any reference to the Charges and Regulations is significant and implies that these sections were not authored by Anderson. Indeed, the Charges are materially at odds with Anderson's Calvinist religious beliefs, something displayed clearly in the 1738 Constitutions.

In fact, Anderson is identified as 'the author of this book' almost as an afterthought on page 74 of the 1723 Constitutions in a line in the middle of the second page of the Approbations. This contrasts with the prominent position given to Senex and Hooke, the co-publishers, whose names appear prominently in the Frontispiece; to Desaguliers, who signs the Dedication; and to Payne, described as the Compiler of the Regulations. Had Anderson fulfilled a more substantive role it would have been conventional for him to have been recognised on the Frontispiece and acknowledged in the Introduction.

According to Anderson's later record, he was instructed by 'His Grace and Grand Lodge' on 29 September 1721 to 'digest the Gothic Constitutions'. A committee was appointed to examine the manuscript, and on 22 March 1722 after 'perusal and corrections' by the past and current Deputy Grand Masters, John Beale and Desaguliers, 'and other learned brethren', the draft

Constitutions was presented to the Duke of Montagu for formal endorsement.

Those described as having approved the book comprise a list of officers and Masters of the constituent lodges falling within the orbit of Grand Lodge. Anderson's name also appears, described as the Master of lodge XVII.

It may be useful to consider why Anderson was willing to act as a hired pen. There were several potential reasons. Anderson's pay from his Swallow Street congregation, a church 'much out of repair', would have been slight. He had probably speculated and lost in the collapse of the South Sea Company in 1720 and was willing to seek out opportunities to earn extra income. And he was known to Desaguliers and Payne as someone who was published, literate, and familiar with Freemasonry.

The Mystery of Masonry brought to Light by the Gormogons
William Hogarth (1724)
Detail – James Anderson is reputedly in the foreground

THE DUKE OF MONTAGU

Desaguliers, George Payne and Martin Folkes were pivotal to persuading John Montagu, 2nd Duke of Montagu, to accept the titular leadership of the Craft, as was one of Montagu's closest friends, Charles Lennox, 2nd Duke of Richmond.

Montagu's installation as Grand Master marked a turning point for English Freemasonry. The event garnered widespread attention and ramped up Freemasonry's ability to attract new members. It also added weight to the authority of the Grand Lodge of England over the rapidly increasing number of Lodges being constituted in London and across provincial England and Wales, with Grand Lodge issuing its first warrant to a subordinate lodge in that year: the warrant of the Lodge of Friendship, now No. 6.

Freemasonry's popularity rose to the extent that whereas in 1720 the annual Grand Feast had been held in a function room above the Goose and Gridiron Alehouse near St Paul's Cathedral, the following year, with Montagu at its head, Grand Lodge was obliged to relocate the event to the more capacious Stationers' Hall to avoid disappointing the several hundred and more who now wished to attend.

The 1723 Constitutions record that 'several Noblemen and gentlemen of the best rank, with Clergymen and learned scholars of most professions and denominations... joined and submitted to take the charges... under our present worthy Grand Master, the most noble Prince, John, Duke of Montagu'.

This was key. Montagu demonstrated that Freemasonry was acceptable morally, intellectually, and politically, and that it could be fashionable and fun. The combination provided a rationale for those of 'the best rank' and 'learned scholars of most professions and denominations' to join the Craft. And many others followed.

John Montagu, 2nd Duke of Montagu (1690-1749)
Mezzotint by John Faber Jr. (1684-1756)
after the portrait by Sir Godfrey Kneller (1646-1723)

Freemasonry offered an intriguing mix. The new Grand Lodge and the 1723 Constitutions supported the state and its authority and simultaneously encouraged and demanded religious tolerance and moral integrity, while Masonic meetings provided a convivial fraternal social setting in which to network and an opportunity for self-improvement from entertaining and educational lectures.

The press took up the story. From the early 1720s, London and provincial newspapers published positive digests of Grand Lodge's Quarterly Communications and gave fulsome details of individual Lodge meetings, feasts, processions and philanthropic works. And these reports were replicated elsewhere, in Ireland, Scotland, and in Britain's overseas colonies.

Montagu was in any event a favourite subject for the nation's newspapers and his activities featured regularly with close to 300 news reports published between 1721-35. They include his loyal address to George I, chief mourner at the funeral of the Duke of Marlborough, his father-in-law, and his eldest daughter's wedding to the Duke of Manchester. Even an excursion along the Thames in a 'large flat-bottom boat' was considered worthy of mention, as was his reward for his wife's lost pet dog.

Montagu proved to be an exceptional choice to become Grand Lodge's first noble Grand Master. He was politically pro-Huguenot and pro-Hanoverian, while his intelligence, wealth and social status made him an aspirational figure.

Montagu's father, the first duke, had been England's ambassador to Louis XIV's France and had witnessed Huguenot persecution at first hand. He was consequently 'a great supporter of the French and other Protestants [driven] to England by the tyranny of their princes'.[3] And there were other connections. Montagu's grandmother, Rachel de Massue, was a Huguenot aristocrat, and the Earl of Galway, one of William & Mary's senior military leaders and another Huguenot, a second cousin.

---

[3] John Macky, *Memoirs of the secret services... during the reigns of King William, Queen Anne, and King George I* (London, 1733).

Desaguliers, Payne and Folkes recognised Montagu as an ideal figurehead for an organisation seeking to elevate its status. And his social, political and military standing acted as a powerful beacon to attract others from his circles and elsewhere.

Montagu had the additional advantage of an intimate involvement with the English Court. He had succeeded his father as Master of the Great Wardrobe, a sinecure that paid over £3,000 a year; officiated as Lord High Constable at the coronation of George I in 1714; and in 1727 carried the sceptre at George II's coronation. And he served as Lord Lieutenant of both Northamptonshire and Warwickshire, in each case from 1715 until his death.

In addition, Montagu held prominent military positions, and not only those that were honorific or a consequence of being Marlborough's son-in-law. And he considered his military standing to be of such importance that he lobbied actively to be appointed to the right roles.

When seeking to become Governor of the Isle of Wight, for example, Montagu commented that he wanted it badly that he might 'again…be a military man, that being a military post'. More conventionally, Montagu raised and financed regiments of Horse and Foot and was Colonel of His Majesty's Own Troop of Horse Guards, the premier cavalry regiment.

He was promoted Major General (1735), Lieutenant General (1739), and the following year became Master-General of the Ordnance.

* * * *

THE DUKE OF WHARTON

Philip, Duke of Wharton (1698-1731)
Unknown Artist, c.1722

Despite Montagu's impact, however, Freemasonry suffered a setback in 1722 with the election as Grand Master of Philip, Duke of Wharton (1698-1734). Wharton had been made a freemason aged twenty-two only a few months after Montagu had been installed as Grand Master, and as *Applebee's Original Weekly Journal* noted on 5 August 1721,

> *the Ceremonies being performed at the King's Arms Tavern... His Grace came Home to his House in the Pall Mall in a white Leathern Apron.*

Wharton was in some ways the opposite to Montagu: an archetypical rebellious youth. But his mercurial approach to life lasted from his teens into adulthood and was at the opposite end of the political and psychological spectrum to his father, a leading supporter of William and Mary and opponent of James II.

Under William III and then Queen Anne, Thomas Wharton had been sworn a Privy Councillor, appointed Comptroller of the Royal Household, and served as Lord Lieutenant of Ireland and as Lord Lieutenant of Oxfordshire and Buckinghamshire. He subsequently became Lord Privy Seal and was granted titles that included Marquess of Catherlough, Earl of Rathfarnam and Baron Trim in the Irish Peerage, and Marquess of Wharton and Marquess of Malmesbury in the English.

Wharton thus had exceptional royal and political connections. Indeed, his godparents included William III and Queen Anne. And when he succeeded in 1715 Wharton gained a substantial inheritance to accompany his titles.

But Wharton rebelled. His Grand Tour in 1716 to satisfy an obligation in his father's Will that he travel to Geneva to continue his religious education was abandoned and Wharton went instead to meet the Pretender, James Stuart, at Avignon, who invested him Duke of Northumberland. This was potentially treasonable and could have been disastrous but was overlooked by London and regarded merely as a youthful misdemeanour. After all, Wharton was only 17.

On his return and despite not having the required age, Wharton was allowed to sit in the Irish Parliament, sworn a Privy Councillor, and as a further incentive to good behaviour was created Duke of Wharton in January 1718.

Wharton took his seat in the House of Lords on attaining his majority in December 1719. He appeared to have mellowed and his speeches were generally pro-government, encouraging a belief that Wharton's dukedom had ensured his loyalty. This was soon proved wrong. Wharton's politics were driven by untrammelled self-interest and he launched an effective, well-publicised attack on the government's handling of the South Sea Company crisis, condemning it as 'dangerous bait which might decoy unwary people to their ruin'. His words were accurate but not altruistic. Wharton had speculated and reputedly lost some £120,000, the equivalent of tens of millions today.

Handsome and intelligent, Wharton was a rake whose interests outside of Parliament involved prostitutes, gambling and mischief making. He co-founded the first Hell Fire Club and in 1721 was proscribed for blasphemy, albeit he denied the charge.

Mercurial and self-obsessed, Wharton chose to usurp rather than succeed Montagu as Grand Master, either to commandeer what he may have perceived as a potentially influential organisation or merely cause a nuisance. But regardless of this and perhaps because of his status and wealth, Wharton was accepted as Grand Master, reluctantly or otherwise, and Desaguliers and other Whigs were present at the Grand Feast on 25 June 1722 that marked his installation.

> *Philip, Duke of Wharton lately made a Brother, tho' not the Master of a Lodge, being ambitious of the Chair, got a number of others to meet him at Stationers Hall 24 June 1722. And having no Grand officers, they put in the Chair the oldest Master Mason… and without the usual*

decent Ceremonials, the said oldest Mason proclaimed aloud Philip, Duke of Wharton, Grand Master of Masons... but his Grace appointed no Deputy nor was the Lodge opened and closed in due Form.

Therefore the noble Brothers and all those that would not countenance irregularities disowned Wharton's Authority, till worthy Brother Montagu heal'd the Breach of Harmony, by summoning the Grand Lodge to meet 17 January 1723 at the King's Arms aforesaid, where the Duke of Wharton promising to be True and Faithful, Deputy Grand Master Beale proclaimed aloud the most noble Prince and our Brother Philip Duke of Wharton, Grand Master of Masons, who appointed Dr Desaguliers the Deputy Grand Master and Joshua Timson and James Anderson Grand Wardens.

A report of the meeting in the *London Journal* 30 June 1722 noted that membership of the Society was then some 4,000. If accurate, and it may not have been, this would have been astonishing in that it represented between a quarter and a third of London's gentry and upper middling and demonstrated a vast increase in membership over the past five years.

Perhaps inevitably, Wharton's appointment proved divisive and his insistence that the musicians at the Grand Feast play the Jacobite song 'Let the King enjoy his own again' was petty and irritated many of those present.

Then let us rejoice, With heart and voice,
There doth one Stuart still remain;
And all sing the tune, On the tenth day of June,
That the King shall enjoy his own again

Wharton's blatant anti-Hanoverian stance was considered offensive by many freemasons. But as Pope later commented, Wharton was 'a fool, with more of wit than half mankind, too rash for thought, for action too refined'. Desaguliers reprimanded Wharton accordingly at the Grand Feast and 'Hanoverian decorum was restored, toasts were drunk to prosperity under the present Administration, and to Love, Liberty, and Science'.

Despite his status, Wharton remained unpopular with the Whig majority in Grand Lodge and his exodus in June 1723 cemented the pro-Hanoverian character of English Freemasonry.

Wharton's *de facto* expulsion occurred the same week that he defended Francis Atterbury, the Jacobite Bishop of Rochester, against a charge of treason in the House of Lords.

And despite Atterbury's censure by Parliament, Wharton brazenly accompanied him for part of his journey into exile and provided him with an extravagant gift: an engraved sword.

This was not an image that Grand Lodge would have wanted to project onto English Freemasonry, nor one with which senior freemasons wished to be associated and the flourish with which Desaguliers signed the Minutes that recorded Wharton's departure 'without ceremony' from Grand Lodge was undertaken with feeling.

Wharton nonetheless continued to hone his anti-Hanoverian rhetoric and shortly afterwards established an anti-government journal, *The True Briton*. He also founded a rival alternative fraternal society, 'The Gormogons':

> *We hear that a Peer of the first Rank, a noted Member of the Society of Freemasons, hath suffered himself to be degraded as a Member of that Society, and his Leather Apron and Gloves to be burnt, and thereupon enter'd himself a Member of the Society of Gormogons, at the Castle-Tavern in Fleet Street.*

Wharton's financial profligacy forced him to sell his assets and compound for his debts in Chancery. However, his pro-Jacobite politics and dissolute lifestyle afforded him limited political, public or judicial support. Wharton was forced to flee England for continental Europe in June 1725 and after a short period in Paris travelled to Madrid where he enlisted in the Spanish army and appeared against the British at Gibraltar.

Despite having done so, Wharton co-signed a petition to Grand Lodge in 1728, by which date the conflict was over, to form a Masonic Lodge in Madrid. Perhaps surprisingly, the petition was granted and a Lodge established by Charles Labelye, a consulting engineer and one of Desaguliers' pupils and acolytes, who became its first Master.

There is a suspicion that the Lodge may have been used to report back to London on Wharton's activities in Spain although Charles Delafaye, the government's spymaster, already had an effective and well-established intelligence network in place in Madrid.

Given his reduced circumstances, Wharton's continuing interest in Freemasonry is perhaps understandable. Its burgeoning reputation in continental Europe offered prestige, and he was a former Grand Master. Moreover, at that point, Wharton was still a duke and hoped to regain political favour with the administration in London. But if so, he failed.

Wharton was outlawed by resolution of Parliament on 3 April 1729 for failing to appear to answer a charge of treason and his titles and property were declared forfeit.

It was the end. Wharton died a pauper at the Cistercian Monasterio de Santa María de Poblet in Catalonia just two years later in 1731. He was thirty-three.

* * * *

THE EARL OF DALKEITH

Wharton's attempt to turn the Craft towards the Jacobites and against the Hanoverian administration had been rebuffed. He was replaced as Grand Master by the Earl of Dalkeith, the Duke of Richmond's cousin and a government supporter. Desaguliers was named Deputy Grand Master and exercised power in Dalkeith's name.

Francis Scott, 5th Earl of Dalkeith and 2nd Duke of Buccleuch, succeeded to his titles in 1724. He was the grandson of the Duke of Monmouth, the eldest illegitimate son of Charles II, who had been beheaded by James II.

Dalkeith was wealthy, well-connected and an ardent Hanoverian. His loyalty was marked with him being sworn to the Privy Council in 1725 and investiture as a Knight of the Thistle, Scotland's premier chivalric order. (Although Dalkeith maintained a house in London he lived principally at his castle on a large estate surrounding the town of Dalkeith, south-east of Edinburgh.)

Dalkeith Castle, Scotland

Dalkeith was declared Grand Master in June 1723 at a meeting of Grand Lodge at which Desaguliers presided as Deputy Grand Master:

> *The Ancient Society of Free and Accepted Masons... assembled to the Number of about 600 at Merchant Taylors' Hall where they unanimously chose the Earl of Dalkeith their Grand Master for the year ensuing.*

The date and place of Dalkeith's initiation as a freemason is unknown but he is listed in the 1723 Constitutions as Master of the Rummer, Charing Cross, lodge XI in the list of lodges. William Stukeley also recorded the duke as being present at the Fountain Tavern Lodge in the Strand on 3 November 1723.

Under Dalkeith's auspices Desaguliers re-established stability and began to centralise control, with Grand Lodge resolving that no new Lodge nor its Master and Wardens would be recognised unless it had been regularly constituted by Grand Lodge:

> *no Brother belonging to any lodge within the Bills of Mortality will be admitted to any lodge as a Visitor unless he be known'; and that 'no Strange Brother, however Skilled in Masonry, will be admitted without taking the Obligation again.*

And other regulations designed to minimise risk were adopted, including one of the best known. Passed in January 1723, Grand Lodge resolved that 'it was not in the power of any body of men to make any Alteration or Innovation in the body of Masonry without the consent first obtained of the Annual Grand Lodge'.

Bar his installation, Dalkeith was present at every meeting of Grand Lodge during his year in office, at the conclusion of which the Duke of Richmond, his cousin, was named as his successor.

THE DUKE OF RICHMOND

Freemasonry's fourth noble Grand Master, the 2nd Duke of Richmond, was feted by the press with over 600 articles published during the ten-year period from his father's death in May 1723 to June 1733, and over 2,300 other entries in later years.

Although Richmond ranked below Montagu in terms of wealth, he was arguably a more popular member of the aristocracy. Like Montagu, he had strong connections to the crown and to Britain's learned societies, including the Royal Society, where Martin Folkes, one of his closest friends, was a Vice President.

Not coincidentally, Richmond appointed Folkes to serve as his Deputy Grand Master.

Richmond's father, the youngest of Charles II's seven illegitimate sons, had been given a dukedom, and Richmond inherited. Born at the family's Goodwood estate, Richmond, like Montagu, was loyally pro-Hanoverian, or as he expressed it: 'bred up from a child in Whig principles'.

Richmond dominated politics in Sussex, with the county returning government supporters to the Commons throughout Richmond's life. He was rewarded accordingly: appointed Aide-de-Camp to George I in 1724 and reappointed by George II; installed a Knight of the Bath in 1725 and a Knight of the Garter in 1726; and granted sinecures that included Lord High Constable of England and Lord of the Bedchamber.

Richmond was raised to the Privy Council in 1735 and appointed a Lord Justice of the Realm in 1740, one of a handful of trusted members of the nobility who exercised executive authority in the name of the crown when the monarch was absent overseas.

Charles Lennox, 2nd Duke of Richmond (1701–1750)
Jonathan Richardson the elder (1667–1745)

Richmond inherited a French dukedom, Aubigny in 1734 on the death of his grandmother. And it was in this context that the duke, accompanied by Desaguliers, established a Lodge in France, No. 133, the following year.

Although Freemasonry in France has been associated with Jacobitism, a number of French freemasons, including Charles Louis de Secondat, Baron Montesquieu, were Anglophiles who favoured the natural liberties and philosophical concepts associated with constitutional government and the rationalism embedded in Newtonian science and culture. At least three Parisian lodges, Louis d'Argent, Villeroy-Coustos, and Bussy Aumont, used anglicized Masonic ritual and held scientific and other lectures similar to those given in English Lodges.

With the election of members and officers and by-laws based on a majority vote, a radical concept in France, such Lodges set a modest political challenge to the autocratic monarch-centred institutions that characterised Louis XV's France.

Richmond's engagement with Freemasonry in France and in the Netherlands was both social and political, and it was given added impetus by his relationship with the Duke of Newcastle, Secretary of State for the Southern Department for over two decades (1724-1748), and with Charles Delafaye, the government's chief spymaster and a fellow member of the Horn Tavern Lodge, for whom it was an effective exercise in soft diplomatic power.

It became customary for Richmond to travel to France each autumn and in September 1735 the *St James's Evening Post* reported that he and Desaguliers had formed a Lodge at the Hotel Bussy in Rue Bussy, Paris:

> *His Grace the Duke of Richmond and the Rev Dr Desaguliers... authorised by the present Grand Master... his Excellency the Earl of Waldegrave, his Majesty's Ambassador to the French King, the Right Hon. the President Montesquieu, the Marquis de Lomaria, Lord*

Dursley, son of the Earl of Berkley... and several other persons, both French and English, were present; and the following noblemen and gentlemen were admitted to the Order: namely, His Grace the Duke of Kingston, the Hon. Count de St. Florentin, Secretary of State to his most Christian Majesty; the Right Hon. The Lord Chewton, son to the Earl of Waldegrave; Mr Pelham, Mr Armiger, Mr Colton and Mr Clement... After which, the new Brethren gave a handsome Entertainment to all the Company.

Freemasonry's clubbable fraternalism was at the core of its diplomatic success and Richmond was an excellent and effective envoy.

He was held in high regard by his contemporaries. Lord Hervey considered that 'there never lived a man of more amiable composition... thoroughly noble in his way of acting, talking and thinking'. And Henry Fielding described him as 'excellent' and as 'one of the worthiest of Magistrates, as well as the best of men'.

In Montagu and Richmond's wake, other young and wealthy aristocrats were encouraged into Grand Lodge and gave their political and social imprimatur to Freemasonry by their public association. They provided a further spur to the expansion of Freemasonry into the gentry, the military, the professions and, perhaps most significantly, among the aspirational middling.

The move launched Freemasonry into the public's consciousness and created within a few years a club whose aspiring members could consider, perhaps justifiably, that they were on the inside of a set that genuinely mattered.

* * * *

FREEMASONRY & THE LONDON MAGISTRACY

Within London Freemasonry were men whose opinions and loyalty mattered, including crown officials, politicians, merchants and military officers. It was no coincidence that many such Hanoverian loyalists served as magistrates. Indeed, twenty-three members of the Horn, around a third of its membership, sat on the Middlesex or Westminster benches.

Among the most senior was Charles Delafaye, a long-serving under-secretary of state and the government's trusted spymaster. Four other members of the Horn had chaired the Middlesex and Westminster benches in successive years: William Cowper, Alexander Chocke, Nathaniel Blackerby and Leonard Streate.

There is no evidence to suggest that the relationship between Freemasonry and the magistracy was interdependent and there was no government or Masonic conspiracy to crowd the bench with freemasons, but many, perhaps most, freemasons were loyal to George I and George II and their governments and precisely the type of men those administrations favoured.

As William Cowper made clear in his *Charge to the Grand Jury of Middlesex*, given in January 1723:

> *It ought always to be a Matter of particular Distinction... that Justices would be vigilant to detect and produce to Punishment all those who... attempt the Subversion of the Great basis upon which stands all that is or can be dear to England and Protestants... It is...for our Religion, our Liberty and our Property.*

The changes made to the composition of the magistracy from 1714 were substantive and successive governments were rigorous in appointing dependable political allies and removing opposition sympathisers. This was above all the case in Westminster and Middlesex where the bench was configured to be explicitly supportive of the administration. In Norma Landau's memorable phrase 'fidelity to the Hanoverian [government was] a touchstone for fitness'.

Supporting this analysis but rarely mentioned by historians, each of the first three Hanoverian Lord Chancellors, William Cowper, 1st Earl Cowper (1714-18); Thomas Parker, 1st Earl of Macclesfield (1718-25); and Peter King, Baron King of Ockham (1725-33), had strong family connections to Freemasonry.

Earl Cowper's nephews included William Cowper, the Grand Secretary and Deputy Grand Master, and his brother, John Cowper, another member of the Horn Tavern Lodge. The Earl of Macclesfield's son, George, was a member of the Duke of Richmond's Lodge at the Swan Tavern in Chichester. And Lord King's son, John, a Grand Steward in 1731, was a member of the Lodge of Antiquity.

The magistracy held a key position in eighteenth-century England. Their work incorporated the preservation of the king's peace and justice, but the bench also ruled on the seriousness of offences brought before it and thus the type and severity of punishment meted out.

In London the magistracy acted as the principal line of defence against the mob and the Quarter Sessions in which they served determined all offences, including treason. The implicit support given to Freemasonry and Grand Lodge by successive administrations was a product of its pro-establishment stance and the positive function that it was deemed to fulfil. And the characteristics of those at its head, especially justices such as Cowper, Delafaye, Streate, Blackerby and Thomas De Veil, reinforced the relationship.

Delafaye had been appointed a magistrate in 1714-15 and remained on the bench for more than two decades. His dependability was such that he became one of the government's principal 'go to' figures for political cases. He adjudicated on hearings that ranged from the committal of a Jacobite sympathiser 'for publicly affirming in St James's Park that the Pretender was the only rightful and lawful King', to investigating plots against the crown: 'persons who were talking of some misfortune that should happen to the King tomorrow as his Majesty should pass over Sandy End Bridge on his way to London'.

Delafaye also took part in Quarter Sessions. That of December 1722, for example, saw him sitting alongside ten others of whom at least six (and possibly seven) were Masonic colleagues, five of whom were fellow members of the Horn Tavern. Such men epitomised Hanoverian loyalty and their presence on the magistrates' bench and in the Lodge provided confirmation to any doubter that Freemasonry could and should be regarded as faithful to the country.

With the government justifiably suspicious of secret gatherings and societies, the Freemasons provided no reasons for concern. Indeed, the Secretary of State, Lord Townshend's eldest son, Charles, a Whig MP, was a member of the Lodge at the Old Devil Tavern in Temple Bar. Charles Delafaye, Townshend's loyal under-secretary of state and chief spymaster, was a member of the Horn Tavern Lodge. John Lefevre, head of the government's Secret Department, was a member of the Lodge at the King's Head, Pall Mall.

Moreover, within the 3,000 or so freemasons whose names recorded by the Grand Lodge of England between 1723 and 1735 there were over one hundred ranking officers, including two later Field Marshals, twenty-three colonels, eight majors and fifty-six captains. This excludes more than sixty aristocrats who financed and commanded their own regiments or who otherwise held field rank.

* * * *

ALEXANDER CHOCKE

Alexander Chocke (d.1737), a senior official at the Exchequer and a Westminster magistrate, served as a Grand Warden in 1726 and succeeded William Cowper as Deputy Grand Master the following year.

Chocke served as Clerk of the Debentures at the Exchequer, a lucrative role yielding some £400 per annum. The position was in the gift of the Earl of Halifax, Auditor of the Exchequer. Chocke had been promoted from Clerk of the Registers and had held office in the department since the turn of the century. His obituary in the *Daily Gazetteer* on 24 January 1737 records 'near forty years' of service. Chocke featured regularly in parliamentary committees with his name recorded often in the *Official Gazette*. Chocke's activities on the Middlesex and Westminster benches were also reported extensively and confirm his support for the government.

Masonically, Chocke was a member of three lodges: the Horn Tavern, close to his home at New Palace Yard; the Swan at Greenwich, where Sir James Thornhill and Joseph Highmore were members; and the Castle Inn in Highgate, where Nathaniel Blackerby was also a member.

Chocke was part of the inner circle at Grand Lodge and was chosen to attend upon the Earl of Dalkeith when the latter was appointed Grand Master and to thank him for his agreement to serve. Being selected for this role was significant and indicates that Chocke was close to Desaguliers. Indeed, Chocke and his wife were godparents to Desaguliers' children.

Chocke was appointed a Grand Warden in 1726 under Lord Inchiquin, with William Cowper appointed as Deputy Grand Master. The following year Chocke became Deputy Grand Master himself under Lord Coleraine, with Blackerby and Highmore as Grand Wardens.

Alexander Chocke, Deputy Grand Master, 1728
Painted in the robes of an Esquire to a Knight of the Bath of which order John, 2nd Duke of Montagu, was Grand Master.

WILLIAM COWPER

William Cowper (*d.*1740), was the first Secretary of the Grand Lodge of England, a pivotal position, and later Deputy Grand Master. With Desaguliers, Payne, and the Dukes of Richmond and Montagu, among others, Cowper was instrumental in forging Freemasonry's pro-Hanoverian credentials.

Cowper was the eldest surviving son of the Hon. Spencer Cowper (1669-1728, Chancellor of the Duchy of Lancaster, Attorney General to the Prince of Wales and Chief Justice of Chester), served as Clerk of the Parliaments with responsibility for the operation of the House of Lords and House of Commons. He advised the Speaker and Members on parliamentary procedure. The position had been held formerly by his uncle, Sir William Cowper, a lawyer and Whig MP; Cowper acquired the reversionary interest in 1715.

Although the role had a relatively nominal salary of £40, Cowper's earnings were supplemented by fees for parliamentary services. These were considerable. In 1717-8, Cowper earned £279 for 'delivering to the Chancery and Rolls Chapel several Acts of Parliament', and a similar amount in connection with private members' bills. And given his responsibility for allocating jobs within Parliament, he received recompense from those he selected. These were sometimes substantial: several of the appointments in his gift commanded salaries of up to £400.

Cowper also occupied senior positions within the London magistracy, posts that were synonymous with the government's imprimatur . He was elected chair of the City of Westminster bench in 1723, a post he held until stepping down in December 1727; and served as chair of the Middlesex County bench in 1729 and again in 1730.

A few months later Cowper was appointed Patentee to the Commission of Bankrupts, a role described by the press as 'very valuable'. He was re-elected to chair the Middlesex bench in 1733 and the same year appointed one of several commissioners charged with a review of the Courts of Justice. Cowper's loyalty to the crown and to the government was beyond doubt and the Charge he delivered to the Grand Jury of Middlesex in January 1723, only a few months before the publication of the Constitutions, provides a particularly apposite example of a loyal address:

> *It ought always to be a Matter of particular Distinction... that Justices would be vigilant to detect and produce to Punishment all those who... attempt the Subversion of the Great basis upon which stands all that is or can be dear to England and Protestants... It is... for our Religion, our Liberty and our Property.*

An address delivered on 30 June 1727 to George II and reported verbatim in the *London Gazette* was similarly clear in its exhortation 'to preserve our current constitution in Church and State'. Another three years later to his fellow magistrates was analogous:

> *The Magistrate... is trusted to uphold the Honour, the Dignity, and the Majesty of the State; to see that Order is observed; that equal Right be done according to known and approved Law; and ever to bear in Mind the high Nature, and vast importance of this Trust; and whoever assumes... such Powers upon any other Principle, is, and should be treated as, a Subverter of Peace, Order, and good Government, of the world, and an Enemy to human Society.*

The parallels with the 1723 Charges are evident. A Freemason would

> *... be a good man and true, and strictly... obey the moral law... be a peaceable subject, and cheerfully to conform to the laws of the country... not be concerned in plots and conspiracies against government; and patiently... submit to the decisions of the supreme legislature [and]... civil magistrate.*

AN

ACCOUNT

OF THE

Swedish and *Jacobite*

PLOT.

WITH

A VINDICATION of our Government from the horrid Aspersions of its Enemies.

AND

A POSTSCRIPT, relating to the *Post-Boy* of *Saturday*, *Feb.* 23.

In a Letter to a Person of Quality, occasion'd by the Publishing of Count Gyllemborg's *Letters.*

LONDON;
Printed for *S. Popping* at the Black Raven in *Pater-noster-Row*, *J. Harrison* at the *Royal-Exchange*, and *A. Dodd* at the Peacock without *Temple-Bar*.
M. DCC. XVII. (Price Six-Pence.)

NATHANIEL BLACKERBY

Similarly at the core of the Grand Lodge of England and its first Grand Treasurer, Nathaniel Blackerby (16..?-1742), served as Clerk of the Patent, a mid-level position at the Exchequer, and as Treasurer to the Commission for Building Fifty Churches, working closely with Nicholas Hawksmoor (1662-1736), the Commission's Principal Surveyor. They were responsible for signing completion certificates, with Blackerby disbursing funds worth the equivalent of tens of millions today. In 1726, William Cowper appointed Blackerby to the sinecure of Housekeeper in Ordinary at Westminster Palace, one of many positions in his gift.

Like Cowper, Desaguliers and Payne, Blackerby was a member of the Horn Tavern Lodge in New Palace Yard. He was also a member of Grand Lodge, serving as Grand Warden in 1727, Deputy Grand Master in each of the following two years, and appointed Grand Treasurer of the Charity Bank, the first to hold that position. Blackerby promoted Freemasonry avidly and in 1729 and again in 1730 wrote the prologue and epilogue for plays performed at the Theatre Royal in Drury Lane in front of a predominantly Masonic audience:

Blackerby was also a London magistrate and following Cowper's resignation as chair of the bench in 1727 was nominated his successor. However, 'after a Letter... intimating his Desire of being excused the chair', Leonard Streate, a member of the Horn who had chaired the bench in 1725, was 'unanimously chose'.

In 1738, shortly after becoming Deputy Lord Lieutenant for Middlesex, Blackerby was nominated to chair the Westminster magistrates' bench once more. On this occasion he accepted and his Charge to the Westminster Justices was similar in that of William Cowper some years before, with Blackerby reminding his audience that 'duty, liberty and property' were fundamental to good society.

JOHN SENEX & JOHN HOOKE: PUBLISHERS

John Senex (1678-1740), an exceptional engraver, cartographer and geographer, was probably the most skilled in eighteenth-century London. He became surveyor and geographer to Queen Anne and produced and sold maps, terrestrial globes, astronomical models and engravings, as well as scientific instruments.

John Hooke (c.1691-1730), a bookseller, stationer and publisher originally apprenticed to Charles Harper of the London Company of Stationers, became a Freeman of the Company in 1712.

Both were active Freemasons, Senex a member of the Lodge at the Fleece Tavern in Fleet Street and a Grand Warden in 1723; and Hooke a Warden at the Fountain Tavern in the Strand. Senex also published Desaguliers' scientific books and in 1728 was sponsored by Desaguliers as a Fellow of the Royal Society.

JOHN PINE: ENGRAVER

The frontispiece of the 1723 Constitutions was engraved by John Pine. Born in London, Pine studied engraving under Bernard Picart in Amsterdam, returning in around 1719 to work as an engraver, printer and publisher of maps and books.

Pine was appointed Bluemantle Pursuivant at the College of Arms and later principal engraver to the Signet and Stamp Office. His work for Grand Lodge included not only the Frontispiece but also the Registers of Lodges, Charity Committee's reports, for which he waived his fees, and the Quarterly Communications. Minutes.

Pine's social circle was wide and included William Hogarth, another prominent freemason. Both were governors of Thomas Coram's Foundling Hospital and advocates for copyright protection, lobbying which found success in the Copyright Act of 1735, the first of its kind.

	King-ſtreet Weſtminſter	every other Mond. from ye 29th of April — inclusive —
	Fleet-ſtreet	last Fryday in every Month
	near Cripplegate	fourth Thursday in every Month
	Charring Croſs	first Thursday in every Month
	in the Strand	fifth Day of the Month
S.t Johnsgate	Clerken Well	every other Tuesd. from Easter Tuesd. inclusive
	Drury-lane	Second Monday in every Month
D B	Southampton ſtreet Covent-Garden	Second Thursday in every Month
	St. Giles's	every other Thursd. from ye 2d. of May inclusive
E C	Charring Croſs	First Fryday in every Month
	Fiſh-ſtreet Hill -	Second Wednsday in every Month
	Southwark	Second Monday in every Month
	Dutchy-lane in the Strand	Second Fryd. in every Month
	Chancery lane	First Monday in every Month
	Clare Market	First Wednesday in every Month
	Pallace-yard Weſtminſter	First & Third Thursday in every Month
	Newgate ſtreet	Second Fryday in every Month
	Ludgate ſtreet	First & Third Wednesday in every Month
	Dyot-ſtreet St. Giles	every other Mond. from ye 22d. of April inclusive
Ben's	New Bond ſtreet	every other Tuesd. from June ye 18th. inclusive
	Bartholomew lane	First Tuesday in every Month
	St. Pauls Church-yard	First Fryday in every Month
	Great Queen ſtreet	First & Third Thursday in every Month
	St. Iohns Wapping	Second Tuesday in every Month

List of Lodges
Engraved by John Pine (1723)

* * * *

THE 1723 CONSTITUTIONS

The 1723 Constitutions' Enlightenment principles provide the philosophical foundations for modern Freemasonry. The Constitutions can be divided into three principal sections: a Traditional History which places Freemasonry within a literary historical context; a set of Charges to which freemasons are expected to adhere, unarguably the most significant component; and General Regulations governing the administration of Grand Lodge and Masonic lodges.

Subsidiary sections include Masonic songs which celebrate the Master of the Lodge, his Wardens, Fellowcraft and Entered Apprentices; and an Approbation listing the Grand Officers and Masters and Wardens of twenty lodges. The book begins with a Dedication to the Duke of Montagu by Jean Theophilus Desaguliers.

The 1723 Constitutions is similar in structure to the Old Charges that governed medieval (and later) stonemasons' lodges. This was intentional. It positioned the Grand Lodge of England as a continuation of that which preceded it, a technique that afforded legitimacy in a tradition-based society.

But the ideas promoted by the Grand Lodge of England were not medieval; they were the opposite, new and materially different.

Moreover, the 1723 Constitutions and Modern Freemasonry were not simply a product of the Enlightenment. They also impacted upon it, not least in acting as a vector for the transmission of Enlightenment principles both nationally and internationally, encouraging 'good and true Men... and of good Report'.

THE CHARGES

At first glance the 1723 Constitutions is broadly similar in structure to the Old Charges in that it comprises a traditional history, a set of charges or injunctions as to belief, and a list of regulations. But the similarity is superficial. Although the form is designed to mirror medieval precedents and add historical gravitas - 'compiling and digesting this Book from the old Records... preserving all that was truly ancient and authentic' - the substance differs materially. And this was intentional.

The Old Charges contain oaths in which Masons swear to be true to God and the Church and profess fealty to the king. The oaths were to a Trinitarian God and the expressions of loyalty and deference to an absolute, divinely appointed monarch. Both speak to a commitment to a 'natural' God-determined social order: 'true to the lord, or Master, that you serve... that his profit and advantage be promoted'. They represent a social and political structure that was once considered immutable.

As the centuries progressed this order was subject to flux, but the oaths nevertheless persisted unaltered and remained the stated credo. And although the purpose of such oaths can be interpreted as providing a form of political insurance and a justification for wage negotiations that were technically illegal, they were nonetheless genuine statements of belief for many.

In contrast, the 1723 Charges and Regulations are based on radical Enlightenment principles that the Grand Lodge of England sought to ensure would be disseminated widely and applied uniformly. This was put into effect via the publication of the 1723 Constitutions – 'for the Use of the Lodges' – and underlined with a declaration that 'all the Tools used in working shall be approved by the Grand Lodge'.

The First Masonic charge – Concerning God and Religion – is a statement in favour of thoughtful personal morality and religious tolerance:

> *A Mason is obliged... to obey the Moral Law... But tho' in ancient times Masons were charged in every Country to be of the Religion of that Country or Nation, whatever it was, yet 'tis now thought more expedient only to oblige them to that Religion in which all Men agree, leaving their particular Opinions to themselves; that is, to be good Men and true, or Men of Honour and Honesty, by whatever Denominations or Persuasions they may be distinguished; whereby Masonry become[s] the Centre and Union, and the means of conciliating true Friendship and Persons that must have remained at a perpetual Distance.*

The charge replaces the former statement of Trinitarian Christian belief with an obligation to 'that Religion in which all Men agree'. In essence, it affirms a belief in a divine being rather than adherence to a specific religious doctrine or church. It is a declaration in favour of religious tolerance and as such sparked attacks on Freemasonry from established churches and religious authorities in several countries, most notably the 1738 Papal encyclical – *In eminenti apostolatus* – which threatened Catholic freemasons with the penalty of excommunication and encouraged the Inquisition to 'investigate and proceed against the transgressors and pursue and punish them'.

The first Masonic Charge made clear that Protestant Dissenters, Catholics and Jews (and Hindus, Zoroastrians, Muslims, and those of other faiths), were welcome in Freemasonry. Indeed, despite the political and religious hostility to Catholicism in eighteenth-century England, Thomas Howard, 8th Duke of Norfolk, England's leading Catholic nobleman, was installed as Grand Master of Grand Lodge in 1729. English Freemasonry was (and is) regarded as a vehicle for religious and social assimilation, a feature that was underlined in the 1700s when many Huguenots who had found religious sanctuary in England chose to join Masonic lodges.

Given that the Charges, Regulations and modified Ritual were designed to promote Enlightenment principles, it is perhaps unsurprising that several key figures involved in their composition were Newtonian natural philosophers who shared a belief in rational observation and interpretation, and who embraced 'the universal Religion or the Religion of Nature'. In their eyes, 'the essential part of religion [was] of an immutable nature because [it was] grounded upon immutable reason... religion may therefore be called the Moral Law of all nations'.

This is an intellectual approach founded on Newtonian principles that unites a belief in a deity with the rational observation of the natural world. Related contemporary texts such as Harcouet de Longeville's *Long Livers* (1722) express a similar approach. Dedicated to the Freemasons and to 'Men excellent in all kinds of Sciences', *Long Livers* proclaims that:

> *it is the Law of Nature which is the Law of God, for God is Nature.*

The concept soon became part of the Masonic mainstream. William Smith's *A Pocket Companion for Freemasons* (1735), declared:

> *As Masons we only pursue the universal Religion or the Religion of Nature. This is the Cement which unites Men of the most different Principles in one sacred Band and brings together those who were most distant from one another.*

Desaguliers, the principal author of the Charges, was a religious latitudinarian, tolerant of others' religious views and not insisting on strict conformity to a particular religious doctrine or set of beliefs. He was also one of the foremost scientific lecturers and Newtonian scholars in the first half of the eighteenth century.

Desaguliers' Enlightenment views were shared by others within Grand Lodge, including Martin Folkes, later President of the Royal Society, and the Dukes of Montagu and Richmond.

The Second Masonic charge – Of the Civil Magistrate Supreme and subordinate – addresses civic responsibility in the context of the political uncertainties that accompanied the Hanoverian succession and the ongoing threat from the exiled James Stuart and his Jacobite supporters. It states that:

> *A Mason is a peaceable Subject to the Civil Powers... never to be concerned in Plots and Conspiracies against the Peace and Welfare of the Nation [and] if a Brother should be a Rebel against the State, he is not to be countenanced in his Rebellion, but he may be pitied as an unhappy Man; and, if convicted of no other Crime, though the loyal Brotherhood must and ought to disown his Rebellion, and give no Umbrage or Ground of political Jealousy to the Government for the time being; they cannot expel him from the Lodge, and his Relation to it remains indefeasible.*

It was a radical concept that a freemason could be 'a Rebel against the State' and although he might be 'disowned' his rebellion would provide insufficient grounds for expulsion in the absence of any crime. The logic follows from the first charge in which 'Masonry [is] the means of conciliating... persons that must have remained at a perpetual distance'. It also referenced the different political views within eighteenth-century English Freemasonry. But, even so, an obligation to pay due obedience to the state is evident and in his formal welcome to the lodge a new Entered Apprentice is enjoined to 'behave as a peaceable and dutiful Subject, conforming cheerfully to the Government under which he lives'.

Although allegiance to an absolute monarch – to be 'a true liege man to the king' – had been at the core of the Old Charges, the new ritual declares that freemasons are subject to the 'supreme legislature': to an elected parliament, independent judiciary, and a constitutional monarch. Desaguliers expresses the concept of an ideal political structure – that 'which does most nearly resemble the Natural Government of our System' – and declares his support for constitutional monarchy in *The Newtonian System of the World*:

> *The Primaries lead their Satellites,*
> *Who guided, not enslav'd, their Orbits run,*
> *Attend their Chief, but still respect the Sun,*
> *Salute him as they go, and his Dominion own.*

Freemasons would no longer be blindly loyal liegemen 'without treason or falsehood' but would instead 'attend' and 'respect', and be 'guided, not enslaved'.

The Third Masonic charge – Of Lodges – reinforces the point that although membership is open, Freemasonry is aspirational:

> *The persons admitted Members of a Lodge must be good and true Men, free-born, and of mature and discreet Age'.*

The sentiment is reinforced by the next charge – Of Masters, Wardens, Fellows and Apprentices – which offers a radical approach to preferment in an age when rank, patronage and precedence was fundamental to social order, and promotion based rarely on merit:

> *All preferment among Masons is grounded upon real Worth and personal Merit only; that so the Lords may be well served, the Brethren not put to Shame, nor the Royal Craft despised... no Master or Warden is chosen by Seniority, but for his Merit.*

The charge continues, emphasising that Freemasonry offers the prospect of advancement or promotion based on experience:

No Brother can be a Warden until he has passed the part of a Fellow-Craft; nor a Master until he has acted as a Warden, nor Grand Warden until he has been Master of a Lodge, nor Grand Master unless he has been a Fellow-Craft before his Election, who is also to be nobly born, or a Gentleman of the best Fashion, or some eminent Scholar, or some curious Architect, or other Artist, descended of honest Parents, and who is of similar great Merit in the Opinion of the Lodges.

The Fifth Masonic charge – Of the Management of the Craft – is a continuation of the long-standing practice of substituting allegorical or 'speculative' uses for operative Masonic tools.

Allegory was a core aspect of Freemasonry after 1723 and is expressed overtly in the explanation of the working tools in each of the three Degree ceremonies.

The Sixth and last charge – Of Behaviour – deals with etiquette and personal conduct, placing civility and morality – 'politeness' – at the heart of personal behaviour for the good of the individual and for society as a whole.

Over the following decades a catechism was added to the Ritual. This remains in use today and requires each Master-elect to give his affirmation to various civic, social and moral obligations that form the essence of the Charges and Regulations. They are set out below:

THE CATECHISM

- To be a good man and true, and strictly to obey the moral law.

- To be a peaceable subject, and cheerfully to conform to the laws of the country in which you reside.

- Not to be concerned in plots and conspiracies against government, but patiently to submit to the decisions of the supreme legislature.

- To pay a proper respect to the civil magistrate, to work diligently, live creditably, and act honourably by all men.

- To hold in veneration the original rulers and patrons of the Order of Masonry, and their regular successors, supreme and subordinate, according to their stations; and to submit to the awards and resolutions of your brethren when convened, in every case consistent with the constitutions of the Order. You agree to avoid private piques and quarrels, and to guard against intemperance and excess.

- To be cautious in carriage and behaviour, courteous to your brethren, and faithful to your Lodge.

- To promote the general good of society, to cultivate the social virtues, and to propagate the knowledge of the art.

In 1738, James Anderson altered the Charges (and other aspects of the Constitutions) in a new edition published in 1738 and written by Anderson alone.

Anderson's changes endured for over a decade but were ultimately not accepted. The Charges were subsequently restored to their original form in the 1756 edition of the Constitutions published by John Entick.

They remained broadly unchanged thereafter.

* * * *

THE GENERAL REGULATIONS

Compiled first by Mr George Payne, Anno 1720, when he was Grand Master, and approv'd by the Grand-Lodge on St John Baptist's Day, Anno 1721, at Stationers' Hall, London; when the most noble Prince John Duke of Montagu was unanimously chosen our Grand-Master for the Year ensuing.

Where the Old Charges contain regulations that protect local trade monopolies and provide a framework for governing an operative or working stonemasons' lodge, Payne's General Regulations differ. Payne, a former Grand Master (1718 & 1720), focuses on the operation of the new Grand Lodge and its constituent (non-operative) lodges, providing an administrative framework for what would become a federal structure for Masonic governance.

Despite an assertion to the contrary, Payne's General Regulations were not a reduction of the 'ancient Records and immemorial Usages of the Fraternity' but a set of rules for a growing and later national and then international organisation. They inculcate Enlightenment philosophical values and reference democratic accountability.

Article 10, for example, states that a 'majority of every particular Lodge, when congregated, shall have the privilege of giving instructions to their Master and Wardens... because the Master and Wardens are their representatives'.

Article 6 requires the unanimous consent of members in respect of any new entrant to the lodge, notwithstanding that this was sometimes observed in the breach.

And although the Grand Master had the right to nominate his successor, if that nominee were not approved unanimously, Articles 23 and 24 specify that members would be balloted.

Taken together, the Charges and Regulations are designed to provide Freemasonry with a robust and enduring philosophical framework and to enhance the ability of Grand Lodge to guard against changes considered inappropriate.

The same principles underpin the ritual and governance framework introduced later in the eighteenth century and in the early nineteenth century – 1813 - when the two previously rival English Grand Lodges – Moderns and Antients – merged to form the United Grand Lodge of England.

General Regulations,

Compiled firſt by Mr. GEORGE PAYNE, *Anno* 1720, when he was **Grand-Maſter**, and approv'd by the GRAND-LODGE on *St. John Baptiſt's* Day, *Anno* 1721, at *Stationer's-Hall*, LONDON; when the *moſt noble* PRINCE *John Duke of* MONTAGU was unanimouſly choſen our **Grand-Maſter** for the Year enſuing; who choſe JOHN BEAL M. D. his *Deputy* GRAND-MASTER; and Mr. *Joſiah Villeneau* and Mr. *Thomas Morris, jun.* were choſen by the Lodge GRAND-WARDENS. And now, by the Command of our ſaid *Right Worſhipful* GRAND-MASTER MONTAGU, the *Author* of this Book has compar'd them with, and reduc'd them to the ancient *Records* and immemorial *Uſages* of the Fraternity, and digeſted them into this new Method, with ſeveral proper Explications, for the Uſe of the Lodges in and about *London* and *Weſtminſter*.

* * * *

THE TRADITIONAL HISTORY

In common with the approach adopted in almost all versions of the medieval Old Charges, James Anderson's account of Freemasonry's development 'from the Beginning of the World' sets a literary context for the Craft. By positioning Freemasonry as an institution that can be dated back to Adam, in Anderson's words, 'our first parent', the narrative gives the Grand Lodge of England a sense of legitimacy, lends it antiquarian status, and offers an aura that a more recently formed organisation would have found difficult to achieve.

Freemasonry's perceived longevity conferred kudos in a society that was heavily tradition-based. Few contemporaries would have taken the history as a literal, truthful record of events. It was then and should now be viewed as falling within a schematic of legend and literary hyperbole. Indeed, a similar approach was followed in the 1750s when the 'The Grand Lodge of England according to the Old Institutions', a rival grand lodge, adopted the name 'Antients' and Laurence Dermott, their Grand Secretary, disparaged the Grand Lodge of England as 'Moderns' in order to underline the Masonic credibility of the younger of the two bodies.

Despite some historians arguing the case, we have commented on the improbability of Anderson being the sole author of the entire 1723 Constitutions as opposed to the version published in 1738. He was nonetheless the author of the traditional history, quantitively the largest component of the Constitutions. However, despite its length and for the reasons given, the history should be viewed as secondary to the Charges and General Regulations which jointly redefined English and later international Freemasonry.

* * * *

THE ENDPIECE – MASONIC SONGS

Celebrated SONGS

In Honour of

MASONRY.

Music was one of the most important forms of recreation in eighteenth-century England. It was at the kernel of social life for people of all income groups and social classes, whether at theatres and concerts, in private venues, or in public gardens and other popular places of resort, such as Vauxhall, or simply in the street and taverns.

Many Londoners of the 'middling sort' could play a musical instrument and everyone was expected to sing. In such circumstances it is unsurprising that music became a popular feature of Masonic meetings. One of the earliest songs, 'The Entered Apprentice's', was written by Matthew Birkhead of the Drury Lane Theatre - a member of the Lodge of Friendship - to a tune which first appeared in 1717.

Masonic meetings were companionable events and partnered by dining, drinking, and smoking. In some lodges this was restricted to periods when the lodge was 'called off'; in others, otherwise. But in both cases there was plentiful time for toasting and singing.

Collections of Masonic songs were published separately and as part of other publications. Indeed, even 'exposures' of supposed Masonic secrets such as *Jachin and Boaz* (1762) contained compilations of 'songs sung at the best Lodges'.

The 1723 Constitutions includes four songs in its endpiece, and Anderson's 1738 Constitutions added several more. Edward Spratt's Irish Constitutions, published in Dublin in 1751, contains

35 pages of songs, and *Ahiman Rezon*, published in 1756, 128 pages of songs and poetry, more than half its length.

Few musical scores were original with most songs set to existing tunes known to many, which was an obvious advantage.

An evening's entertainment may also have featured non-Masonic songs, including some of the more jingoistic of the day such as 'Britons Strike Home', 'Rule Britannia', 'See the Conquering Hero Comes', and 'Hearts of Oak', each to be concluded with a robust toast and Masonic fire.

By design or otherwise, Masonic songs and music reinforced Lodge camaraderie while allying Freemasonry with tradition and history:

Who can unfold the Royal Art?
Or sing its Secrets in a Song?
They're safely kept in Mason's Heart,
And to the ancient Lodge belong.

As a testament to their popularity, in 1731, less than eight years after the publication of the 1723 Constitutions, Bernard Creake, a leading London bookseller, believed it worthwhile to print a volume containing nothing but Masonic songs: *A Curious Collection of the Most Celebrated Songs in Honour of Masonry*. The publication was a great commercial success.

THE
MASTER'S SONG:
OR, THE
HISTORY of *MASONRY*.

MARTIN CLARE

Martin Clare (c.1689-1751), one of London's most influential freemasons in the decades after the publication of the 1723 Constitutions, encapsulates Desaguliers and Payne's remoulded English Freemasonry. Clare was appointed a Grand Steward in 1734, Junior Grand Warden in 1735, and Deputy Grand Master in 1741. He was also a leading member of the King's Arms Lodge in the Strand (the 'OKA') where he was Senior Warden and deputy to the often-absent Sir Cecil Wray, the Master. Clare was in addition Master of the Lodge at the Shakespeare's Head in St James's, where fourteen members hailed from the OKA, and attended other Lodges. However, Clare is known best as an educator and the author of *A Defense of Masonry*, published in 1730 in response to Samuel Prichard's 'exposure', *Masonry Dissected.* Clare's retort was so popular that it was reprinted in full in *Read's Weekly Journal* on 24 October the same year.

Clare was a prolific and popular Masonic lecturer. Although only a few Lodge Minute Books dating back to the early eighteenth century survive, those that do suggest that it was customary in at least some lodges for members to share their knowledge through talks and lectures. The first surviving OKA Minute Book underlines this, recording thirty-six lectures given by members in the decade to 1743. They include seven on human physiology, some of which involved dissections; five which covered different aspects of architecture; more than ten examining scientific inventions, apparatus and industrial processes; while other talks explored art, history and mathematics, among other topics.

Clare was the driving force behind the programme and had been one of London's leading educators for almost two decades. He had been the proprietor of The Soho Academy, one of London's leading boarding schools, since 1717, and his textbook, *Youth's Introduction to Trade and Business* (1720), ran to twelve editions. Clare summed up his approach to education as one that was centred on 'practicality', making sure his charges were 'fitted for business'. He did so by combining the sciences with the social graces, setting the pattern for eighteenth-century British education.

The Soho Academy was one of England's most celebrated and successful private boarding schools and Clare attracted students from many well-connected families. They included John Murray, later 3rd Duke of Atholl; John Christopher Smith, the composer; and the sons of politicians such as Arthur Onslow, the Speaker of the House of Commons.

Clare's approach to Masonic education was in the same vein. He noted in his *Discourse* given to the Grand Stewards' Lodge and then to the Quarterly Communication of Grand Lodge held on 11 December 1735 that

> *the chief pleasure of society – viz., good conversation and the consequent improvements – are rightly presumed... to be the principal motive of our first entering into then propagating the Craft... We are intimately related to those great and worthy spirits who have ever made it their business and aim to improve themselves and inform mankind. Let us then copy their example that we may also hope to attain a share in their praise.*

The *Discourse* was reprinted widely and incorporated into successive editions of the *Pocket Companion for Freemasons* and in translations overseas. Clare based it in large part on John Locke's *Some Thoughts Concerning Education* (1693) and invoked the idea of 'inward civility of the mind', arguing that a freemason should have an Enlightenment perspective that is guided by respect and concern for others, both in and out of lodge:

> *Men, whatever they are guilty of, would not chuse to have their Blemishes displayed and set in open View. Failings always carry some*

Degree of Shame with them; and the Discovery, or even Imputation of any Defect, is not borne by them without Uneasiness.

Moreover, as Clare noted,

We are, let it be considered, the Successors of those who reared a Structure to the Honour of Almighty God, the Grand Architect of the World, which for Wisdom, Strength and Beauty, hath never yet had any Parallel.

We are intimately related to those great and worthy Spirits, who have ever made it their Business and their Aim to improve themselves, and to inform Mankind. Let us then copy their Example, that we may also hope to obtain a Share in their Praise.

This cannot possibly be done in a Scene of Disorder: Pearls are never found but when the Sea is calm; and silent Water is generally deepest.

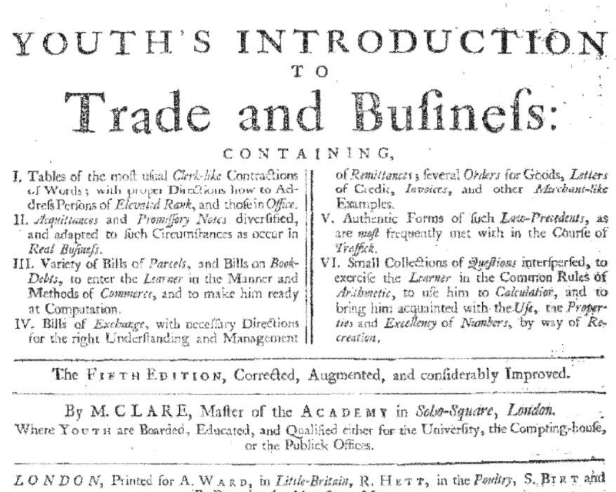

YOUTH'S INTRODUCTION
TO
Trade and Bufinefs:

CONTAINING,

I. Tables of the moft ufual *Clerk-like* Contractions of Words; with proper Directions how to Addrefs Perfons of *Elevated Rank*, and thofe in *Office*.

II. *Acquittances* and *Promiffory Notes* diverfified, and adapted to fuch Circumftances as occur in *Real Bufinefs*.

III. Variety of Bills of *Parcels*, and Bills on *Book-Debts*, to enter the *Learner* in the Manner and Methods of *Commerce*, and to make him ready at Computation.

IV. Bills of *Exchange*, with neceffary Directions for the right Underftanding and Management of *Remittances*; feveral *Orders* for Goods, *Letters* of Credit, *Invoices*, and other *Merchant-like* Examples.

V. Authentic Forms of fuch *Law-Precedents*, as are *moft* frequently met with in the Courfe of *Traffick*.

VI. Small Collections of *Queftions* interfperfed, to exercife the *Learner* in the Common Rules of *Arithmetic*, to ufe him to *Calculation*, and to bring him acquainted with the *Ufe*, the *Properties* and *Excellency* of *Numbers*, by way of *Recreation*.

The FIFTH EDITION, Corrected, Augmented, and confiderably Improved.

By M. CLARE, Mafter of the ACADEMY in *Soho-Square*, *London*.
Where YOUTH are Boarded, Educated, and Qualified either for the Univerfity, the Compting-houfe, or the Publick Offices.

LONDON, Printed for A. WARD, in *Little-Britain*, R. HETT, in the *Poultry*, S. BIRT and B. DOD in *Ave-Mary-Lane*, MDCCXLI.

Martin Clare, *Youth's Introduction to Trade and Business* (1751 edition)

THE

MOTION of FLUIDS,

NATURAL and ARTIFICIAL;

In particular that of the

AIR and WATER,

In a ſamiliar Manner, propoſed and proved, by evident and concluſive EXPERIMENTS with many uſeful REMARKS.

DONE

With ſuch *Plainneſs* and *Perſpicuity*, as that they may be underſtood by the UNLEARNED.

For whoſe Sake there is added,

A Short EXPLANATION of ſuch UNCOMMON TERMS, which in Treating on this SUBJECT could not, without Affectation, be avoided.

With plain DRAUGHTS

Of ſuch EXPERIMENTS and MACHINES, which, by Deſcription only, might not readily be comprehended.

By M. CLARE, *A.M. F.R.S.*

LONDON:
Printed in the YEAR M,DCC,XXXV.

IRELAND

The introduction to Ireland of what is recognised as Modern Freemasonry lagged developments in England by some four years. Nonetheless, Dublin press reports of the Duke of Montagu's decision to accept the position of Grand Master of the Grand Lodge of England in 1721 attracted broad interest across the political spectrum and featured in both pro-government and opposition newspapers. John Whalley's loyalist *Dublin News Letter* carried a description of Montagu's installation in July 1721; and responding to his readers' interests, the following month John Harding's opposition-leaning *Dublin Impartial News Letter* gave an account of the initiation of Viscount Hinchingbroke, Sir George Oxenden and Sir Robert Rich at the King's Arms tavern at St Paul's Churchyard.

The Irish press also reported the Duke of Wharton's decision to join the Craft, with Irish newspapers alerting their readers that 'his Grace [Wharton] was admitted into the Society of Freemasons… and came home to his house in the Pall Mall in a white leather apron'. Despite selling his Irish estates to fund his investment in South Sea Company stock, Wharton had a following in Ireland and was friends with many within the Anglo-Irish aristocracy, including Richard Parsons, 1st Earl of Rosse, subsequently the first Grand Master of the Grand Lodge of Ireland.

In Ireland, as in England, Freemasonry was led publicly by the aristocracy. Born in Twickenham to the west of London, Rosse had succeeded his father as Viscount Rosse in the Irish peerage in 1702 and at the age of twenty-two was created an Earl by George I to encourage and reward his loyalty. He was appointed Grand Master of Ireland in 1725. There is no information as to those holding office at the Grand Lodge of Ireland from 1726-30 and Rosse may have remained at the head of Irish Freemasonry until 1731 when Lord Kingston became Grand Master.

Rosse had rank, celebrity, and extensive connections. His family had been in Ireland and active in its administration since Elizabeth I.

And he had a similar background and character to many of the aristocrats who became figureheads for the Grand Lodge of England: young and affluent, they were willing to act as beacons to prospective members and imbued Freemasonry with a combination of social exclusivity and political protection.

However, like the Duke of Wharton, Rosse was also a libertine whose fortune was directed principally towards personal pleasure. Following a Grand Tour of Europe and Egypt from 1731-35, he established a Hell Fire Club in Dublin where wealthy young Protestant rakes could drink, whore and gamble. But notwithstanding such excesses, Rosse was also a loyal Hanoverian and his Grand Officers, the Hon. Humphrey Butler (DGM), Sir Thomas Prendergast (SGW), Marcus Anthony Morgan (JGW) and Thomas Griffiths (GS), equally loyal.

Although some historians have argued that the Grand Lodge of Ireland in its formative years was the subject of a struggle for dominance between Irish Jacobites and pro-Hanoverian Whigs, and that Irish Freemasonry as a whole was split accordingly, there is slight evidence to support that contention. Indeed, the opposite appears to have been the case with Irish Freemasonry reflecting the ascendancy of the Protestant Anglo-Irish elites.

The Irish press published regular reports on English Freemasonry throughout the 1720s, noting for example the appointment of Richmond as Grand Master in 1724 and Martin Folkes as his deputy. Exposés were also published in Dublin, including *The Grand Mystery of the Free-Masons Disclosed*, as was a riposte, *The Free-Masons Vindication, being an Answer to a Scandalous Libel*. And copies of the 1723 Constitutions were advertised widely and sold by Dublin's booksellers throughout the mid-1720s and into the 1730s.

Frontispiece
Ahiman Rezon (1764)

The driving force behind the formation of the Grand Lodge of Ireland and the participation of Dublin's aristocrats, gentry and professional classes was a desire to emulate the celebrity of the Grand Lodge of England.

The first evidence of a Grand Lodge appears in June 1725 in *The Dublin Weekly Journal*, which published a lengthy account of Rosse's appointment as Grand Master. The report covers almost a full page and describes the procession, installation and subsequent Grand Feast, recording that

> *above a 100 gentlemen' met at the Yellow Lion in Warborough Street and 'after some time putting on their aprons, white gloves and other parts of the distinguishing dress of that Worshipful Order... proceeded over Essex bridge to the Strand and from thence to the King's Inns.*

The parade included the Masters and wardens of 'six lodges of gentleman freemasons... under the jurisdiction of the Grand Master', and after 'marching round the walls of the great hall... the grand lodge, composed of the Grand Master... Grand Wardens and the masters and wardens of the lodges, retired to the room prepared for them where... they proceeded to the election of a new Grand Master etc'.

The article continues, recording that after dinner, 'they all went to [a] play, with their aprons etc., the private brothers sat in the pit, but the Grand Master, Deputy Grand Master and Grand Wardens, in the government's box.' The report is written in a style that implies that the Grand Lodge of Ireland had been in existence for some time, albeit that the opposite was probably correct. And although modelled on the Grand Lodge of England, there were points of difference with the method of installation, most notably the election of the Grand Officers by the members of Irish Grand Lodge as a whole rather than their appointment by the Grand Master.

There are no further references to the Grand Lodge of Ireland and few others regarding Irish Freemasonry until March 1731, when *The Dublin Weekly Journal* published a report of a lodge meeting held on 6 March. This took place at the Yellow Lyon Tavern in Warborough Street once again. *The Journal* recorded that Earl Rosse, Grand Master, the Hon William Ponsonby, worshipful master, and his two wardens, William Cooper and Rowly Hill, were present. Other attendees included Lord Kingston, the past Grand Master of the Grand Lodge of England; the Earl of Drogheda; Lord Southwell; and Thomas Griffith, the Grand Secretary. *The Journal* went on to note that 'upon proper application, the Rt Hon. the Lord Tyrone, the Rt Hon. the Lord Netterville, the Hon. Tho. Bligh, Esq.; and the Hon. Henry Southwell, Esq.; were in due form, admitted members of that Ancient and Right Worshipful Society'.

Irish press reports on English Freemasonry, its initiations, feasts, processions, and its various charitable activities, suggests that the subject remained of significant interest, as does the publication of Pennell's Irish Constitutions in 1730.

Pennell, afterwards Grand Secretary of the Grand Lodge of Ireland, had advertised in *Faulkner's Dublin Chronicle* for a minimum of two hundred subscribers and achieved this goal without difficulty. His work contains a small number of differences in Masonic ritual when compared to the form practiced in London and may have reflected the then current practice in Ireland. The variations include the form of prayer at initiation and the role of deacons, who would have been the stewards of the lodge in England. Over time these and other relatively minor discrepancies would come to be treated as more substantive.

An enduring mark of Irish Freemasonry from the 1750s was its strong relationship with the London-based Antients Grand Lodge. This was cemented by the appointment of the Earl of Blessington, Grand Master of Ireland (1738-39), a leading Irish peer, as the Antients' first noble Grand Master, serving from 1756-60. At the same time, the Antient's Grand Secretary, Laurence Dermott's *Ahiman Rezon* displaced Pennell's Constitutions and the 1723 Constitutions on which it was based to become the preferred version of the Irish Constitutions.

SCOTLAND

Masonic lodges were arguably more visible in Scotland than England and Ireland in the seventeenth and early eighteenth centuries. Scottish lodges can point to well documented histories with some 30 lodges present in Edinburgh, Glasgow, Stirling, Dunfermline, Dundee, Aberdeen, Perth, Dunblane, and Inverness. They comprised working masons and were part of the fabric of Scottish towns whose councils regulated such trades and issued charters of incorporation, also known as 'Seals of Cause'. The Incorporation of Wrights and Masons of Edinburgh, for example, received its Seal of Cause in October 1475; the organisation later became known as 'Mary's Chapel' and is considered one of Scotland's earliest lodges. The position was similar in England, although documentation is less well ordered.

Formal regulation of the mason trade and operative lodges in Scotland began at the end of the sixteenth century when the King's Master of Works, William Schaw of Sauchie, promulgated statutes and regulations for Scottish operative masons. Around a half century later (and perhaps earlier), Scottish lodges began to admit notaries to serve as clerks and non-operative members of the local gentry and merchants who acted as patrons to subsidise the expense of running the lodge. A similar pattern is found in England.

The 1707 Acts of Union which bound Scotland to England to create the United Kingdom of Great Britain brought about wholesale changes to Scotland and shifted the centre of power from Edinburgh to London. One effect was to advance the spread of ideas and thoughts emanating from London, in particular the Enlightenment principles and Newtonian science of the Royal

Society. There was also a tendency to emulate London Society in other ways, especially among the mainly Protestant Whiggist pro-Hanoverian landowners and aristocrats of the Lowlands and West Coast, many of whom had residences in Edinburgh and London.

Iain McIntosh has argued that there is evidence within Scottish Lodge records that a more recognisable form of 'Modern Freemasonry' emerged after the 1715 Jacobite Rising through to the creation of the Grand Lodge of Scotland in 1736. This form of 'gentlemanly' Freemasonry emulated that which had emerged in London. That Scotland did not form its own Grand Lodge until 1736, after England (1717) and Ireland (1725), may highlight the relatively independent and operative nature of Scottish Lodges. Indeed, this is substantiated by the process by which the Grand Lodge of Scotland was formed.

The idea of a Grand Lodge of Scotland was initially promoted by four fashionable Edinburgh-based lodges whose members were predominantly gentlemen: the Lodge of Edinburgh, No.1; Canongate Kilwinning, No.2; Leith Kilwinning; and Kilwinning Scots Arms. Invitations went out to 100 Scottish lodges, of which 33 were represented in 1736 at the inaugural meeting of the Grand Lodge of Scotland. The majority of Scottish Lodges were not supportive and preferred to remain independent. This began to change when lodges were assigned numbers to reflect their relative age, a process that commenced in 1737 based on 'proofs' of documents and artefacts that established lineage and antiquity. McIntosh comments that 'following the publication of the roll, there was a rush from other Scottish Lodges to join, each producing documents etc., of the age of the Lodge, and there resulted a jostle to prove an early foundation and claim a lower, more senior number'.

Scottish Lodges at this time recognised a two-degree system, Apprentice and Fellow Craft, and the 'Mason word' was the principal secret alluded. The first mention of a third Degree does not occur until 1726, when it is recorded in the minutes of Lodge

Dumbarton Kilwinning. It spread quickly but not universally thereafter, mentioned in 1728 in Lodge Greenock Kilwinning, by Lodge Kilwinning in 1735, Canongate Kilwinning in 1736, and the Lodge of Edinburgh in 1738.

Although there was no formal relationship between the Grand Lodge of England and the Grand Lodge of Scotland, there were many personal connections between Scottish aristocrats, politicians and academics and their counterparts in England. Moreover, many Scottish noblemen were Members of Parliament with properties in London. They were also prominent members of London Society and participated actively in fraternal life in the capital, including the Royal Society and Masonic lodges, both of which were highly fashionable.

A plethora of Scottish aristocrats were Grand Masters of the Grand Lodge of England including Francis Scott, 5th Earl of Dalkeith, 2nd Duke of Buccleuch, GM 1723, a Scottish representative peer and a Fellow of the Royal Society; James Hamilton, 7th Earl of Abercorn, GM 1725, also an FRS; James Lyon, 7th Earl of Strathmore, GM 1733, also FRS; John Lindsay, 20th Earl of Crawford, GM 1734, also FRS; John Keith, 3rd Earl of Kintore, GM 1740 & GM of Scotland 1738-39; and James Douglas, 14th Earl of Morton, GM 1741 & GM of Scotland 1739-40, President of the Royal Society (1764) The positon reversed in the second half of the century and from the 1760s many Grand Masters of Scotland associated instead with Antients Freemasonry.

* * * *

NORTH AMERICA

The first Masonic lodges in America were initially in the larger trading centres, principally Boston, Philadelphia, New York, Charleston, and Savannah, locations with strong commercial and social links to England. Freemasonry then took root in other trading and administratrive hubs across the thirteen colonies, with the number of those joining rising substantially. Indeed, Freemasonry became so popular among the elites and middling that in 1734 Benjamin Franklin considered it a sensible financial investment to reprint verbatim the 1723 Constitutions. Franklin's version was sold in Philadelphia and elsewhere, including Charleston and Boston.

In essence the first American Freemasonry was English Freemasonry and it was this that provided the underpinnings for growth over the next three decades. But from the 1760s another structure was overlaid. This was Antients Freemasonry, the seeds of which were spread via the migration of Scots-Irish and London Irish principally to Pennsylvania and from there across the American Frontier. The development created a new kind of American Freemasonry, largely in the form we see today.

When one pictures the Irish diaspora in America, the quintessential images are those of a Boston policeman or Philadelphia firefighter, the Chicago River dyed green on St Patrick's Day and marked elsewhere by green and white parades in cities across America. These images are a testament to the more than four million mainly Southern Irish who dominated nineteenth- and twentieth-century migration to the United States and whose legacy resonates today.

But the pattern of eighteenth-century Irish migration was fundamentally different. An estimated 350-400,000 Irish migrated to North America between 1720 and 1800. They included Catholics, Quakers, and Anglicans, but by far the largest component, well over three-quarters, were Presbyterians – Scots-Irish – the majority from Ulster.

Although the number of eighteenth-century Irish migrants is modest when compared to the millions who arrived over the following two centuries, it is significant nonetheless and equated to around 10% of America's white population which in 1790, at the time of the first census, stood at around 3.2 million.

Many Irish had migrated initially to England – 'the closest place that wasn't Ireland' – and from there sailed to America. Others sailed directly. Those with agricultural leases or businesses that had value sold up and used the proceeds to fund their fares to America and acquire land. Those that could not travelled as indentured labourers, working for up to five years to pay-off their debts. They departed from London, Bristol, and Liverpool, and from Belfast, Londonderry, and Dublin, and from Ireland's minor ports, with destinations that included Charleston, Baltimore, New York and Boston, but especially Philadelphia, the first port of call for the vast majority of Irish migrants.

A minority of Scots-Irish migrants were already freemasons when they arrived in America. Others were initiated into Freemasonry afterwards. And as they moved west to settle the backcountry of Pennsylvania and Virginia, and south and west along the wagon trails into the Piedmont where they would comprise around half the settler population, they carried their Freemasonry with them or embraced it on arrival.

In summary, for most of the period from around 1730 through to the late 1750s and early 1760s, Freemasonry was a relatively elite organisation with members drawn largely from planters, merchants, government officials, lawyers, and other prominent settlers.

Freemasonry in Pennsylvania, for example, brought together many of the city and province's most eminent men and membership of the lodge was viewed as a badge of gentility and cultivation. Indeed, in the late 1740s, some 90% of Philadelphia's freemasons were merchants, professional men, shipowners, and successful artisans, described by historians as the 'creators of the political, intellectual, literary and cultural life of colonial Philadelphia'.

The same was true of Freemasonry and freemasons across the other colonies, not least in Massachusetts, Virginia, South and North Carolina, and Georgia, where the social, financial and political standing of members was mirrored in those chosen to serve as Provincial Grand Masters.

Benjamin Smith, for example, Provincial Grand Master of South Carolina and subsequently PGM of both South and North Carolina, was one of South Carolina's most successful merchant traders and factors, with a client base that stretched across both Carolinas and a business that included exporting naval stores, deerskins and agricultural products, and importing dry and manufactured goods, wine and spirits, and, less admirably, the slave trade. Smith's commercial success was mirrored in politics. Elected to the House of Assembly in 1746, Smith served as Speaker from 1755-63. In 1760, he was offered but declined membership of South Carolina's Royal Council.

The Provincial Grand Master of Virginia, Presley Thornton, a planter and slave owner whose family had migrated to the colony in the 1640s, represented Northumberland County in the House of Burgesses almost continuously until 1760, when he was appointed to the Royal Council. Thornton was among the colony's most affluent citizens and enjoyed a lifestyle typical of an eighteenth-century Virginia plantocrat: horse racing, gambling, sailing, and membership of elite fraternal societies, including Freemasonry.

Joseph Montfort, Provincial Grand Master of North Carolina, a merchant-trader and landowner, led the construction and development of Halifax Town. His focus was not limited to building the physical infrastructure but included raising the town's commercial and social profile. It is in this context that his drive to establish a Masonic lodge at Halifax Town can best be understood. Freemasonry was a mark of sophistication and the lodge a space for gentlemanly association. Montfort gifted the lodge a property lot on which to construct a purpose-built Masonic Hall and in 1769 led a fundraising among members of the lodge that generated over £100, a vast sum at the time.

Other PGMs had similar wealth and position. George Harison, the Provincial Grand Master of New York, the son of Francis Harison, a Lincoln's Inn-educated lawyer and former member of the Governor's Council, benefited from his father's connections and gained appointment as Searcher and Surveyor for New York, a position that put him second-in-command at the Customs Office. It was a pivotal role. New York was one of America's most important ports and an entrepôt for trans-shipping goods to and from Britain, the Caribbean, Canada, and along America's eastern seaboard. And Sir John Johnson, the last PGM of New York, the son and principal heir to Sir William Johnson, was among the largest landowners in the province of New York with land holdings across the Mohawk Valley that exceeded 400,000 acres.

But although early American Freemasonry had followed English (especially London) practice, in the run-up to Independence (post-1765), and throughout the war itself, Freemasonry altered. Many Moderns Freemasons who were loyalists were forced to flee America either during or after the war, while others who remained faced fines or the confiscation of their assets and social opprobrium. In contrast, many notable American patriots were associated with Antients Freemasonry.

Following the War, the lodge became a preferred space for the new nation's leaders. Freemasonry in America was viewed as a font of Enlightenment virtues, high moral principles, and an organisation that worked for the benefit of the community as a whole. This latter aspect was made tangible at the dedication of new public buildings and monuments from the Capitol Building in Washington where the foundation stone was laid by George Washington, the nation's first President and an Antients Freemason, to the University of North Carolina at Chapel Hill where General William Richardson Davie, Grand Master of Freemasons in the state, a war hero and national and state politician who had helped frame the U.S. Constitution, presided over the Masonic ceremony of laying the cornerstone.

Based on such foundations, Freemasonry flourished, its members drawn from the elites and the middling, whether farmers, merchants, storekeepers, tavern owners, bankers or lawyers. And it was that accessibility and inclusiveness that changed the social and political demographics of American Freemasonry.

American Freemasonry evolved further with the the inception of Prince Hall – Black – Freemasonry, when Prince Hall (c.1738-1807), and fourteen other African Americans were accepted as initiates into lodge No. 441 (Irish Constitution) attached to the 38th Regiment of Foot, then stationed at Castle William (now Fort Independence) on Castle Island, Boston. Prince Hall and his colleagues were subsequently granted a warrant by the Grand Lodge of England and the lodge entered onto the Grand Register as African Lodge No. 459. Prince Hall Freemsonry would later expand across the United States and into the Caribbean.

Mid-Eighteenth-century Masonic Working Tools

PRINCE HALL FREEMASONRY

The origin of African Lodge, America's first black Masonic lodge, dates to c.1778 and to Prince Hall (c.1738-1807), a prominent black leader in Boston, Massachusetts. Hall was a staunch proponent of equal treatment and education for blacks, and the abolition of slavery and the slave trade. His additional legacy to Masonic history came when Prince Hall and fourteen other free black men were initiated on 6 March 1778 by Sergeant John Batt and formed African Lodge No.1. Batt was a member of Lodge No. 441, Irish Constitution, which was attached to the 38th Regiment of Foot in the British Army. The regiment was stationed in Boston; it subsequently left for Nova Scotia and New York.

On 2 March 1784, Prince Hall petitioned the Premier Grand Lodge of England with the help of William Moody, Worshipful Master of the Lodge of Brotherly Love, No. 55, in London, England, for a warrant. The arrangements are set out in a letter and petition sent by Hall to Moody:

> *Permit me to return you my hearty thanks for your brotherly courtesy to Brothers Reed and Mene, when in a strange land, and when in a time of need you were so good as to receive them as brothers and to treat them as kindly as they inform me you did. What you have done to them, I look upon as done to me and the whole of us, for which I give you many thanks and likewise to all the Lodge. I hope they behaved themselves as men and as Masons with you, if not I would be glad if you would be so good as to let me know of it and they shall be dealt with accordingly.*
>
> *Dear Brother, I would inform you that this Lodge has been founded almost this eight years, and had no warrant yet but only a permit from Grand Master Rowe to walk on St John's Days and to bury our dead in form which we now enjoy. We have had no opportunity till now of applying for a warrant though we were pressed upon to send to France for one, but we refused it for reasons best known to ourselves.*

We now apply to the fountain from whom we received lights for this favor and, dear Sir, I must beg you to be our advocate for us by sending this, our request, to His Royal Highness, the Duke of Cumberland, Grand Master, and to the Right Honourable Earl of Effingham, Acting Grand Master, the Deputy Grand Master and Grand Wardens and the rest of the Brethren of the Grand Lodge, that they would graciously be pleased to grant us a charter to hold this Lodge as long as we behave up to the spirit of the constitution.

This, our humble petition, we hope His Highness and the rest of the Grand Lodge will graciously be pleased to grant us there, though poor yet sincere Brethren of the Craft. And therefore, in duty bound ever to pray, I beg leave to subscribe myself your loving friend and Brother – Prince Hall, Master of the African Lodge No. 1, June 30th 1784, in the year of Masonry 5784, in the name of the whole Lodge.

C. Underwood, Secretary

In common with most American lodges, African Lodge met sporadically during the War of Independence and, post-war, Hall sought to legitimize its status with recognition from other Boston lodges. They declined, either through racism and/or because they viewed African Lodge as irregular. Frustrated, Hall petitioned the Grand Lodge of England for a warrant.

The petition was delivered to William Moody who passed it to Grand Lodge. It was accepted and African Lodge obtained a charter remarkably quickly on 29 September 1784 and was entered onto the Grand Register as No. 459. There were however problems in arranging for the fee to be delivered to London and the warrant was delayed and not received by Boston until 29 April 1787. African Lodge met a week later on 6 May 1787.

Following the grant of the Lodge's charter, a stream of letters flowed between Boston and London, beginning in 1785 with a formal letter of thanks to the Duke of Cumberland. Between 1787 and 1789, Hall's letters to Rowland Holt, Deputy Grand Master, and William White, Grand Secretary, update London and contain details of initiations, expulsions, and the deaths of various members. There are also requests to acknowledge receipt of their donations to the Grand Charity and a forwarded copy of African Lodge's General Regulations dated 5 January 1789. Most letters were written by Hall personally from his rooms at the Sign of the Golden Fleece on Water Street in Boston.

After the merger of the Antients and Moderns Grand Lodges in Massachusetts on 5 March 1792, African Lodge became the only lodge in Massachusetts that had been constituted by and remained subordinate to the Grand Lodge of England. Unrecognized by any other lodge in Massachusetts, African Lodge regarded itself and was regarded by London as an English Constitution lodge and cemented its status by continuing to contribute to the Grand Charity. This was recognized formally at the April 1792 Quarterly Communication of the Grand Lodge of England.

African Lodge was renumbered No. 370 in 1792 and continued to correspond with and pay fees to London until at least 1797. The lodge remained on the Grand Register until 1813, when creation of the United Grand Lodge of England led to the wholesale erasure of lodges with which London had deemed it had lost contact. Ironically, African Lodge was unaware that it had been renumbered and no longer listed on the Grand Register and in 1824 wrote to London petitioning for the renewal of its charter. The letter acknowledged that while no monies had been sent for some years due to mismanagement, they would now be sending funds across, including the fee for a replacement warrant.

As Worshipful Master of African Lodge, No. 459, Hall initiated several men of colour into masonry and spread this opportunity as far as Philadelphia, Pennsylvania, where new lodges were created under his guidance and leadership. In March 1797, Hall constituted a sister lodge in Philadelphia to work under No. 459's charter and in June the same year warranted another lodge at Providence, Rhode Island, on the same basis. Prince Hall died in 1807 but his historical contributions remain clear.

In 1827, African Lodge No. 459 declared itself to be an independent Grand Lodge with the name African Grand Lodge of Massachusetts, later renamed Prince Hall Grand Lodge of Massachusetts. Prince Hall Grand Lodges are mostly descended from what is now the Prince Hall Grand Lodge of Massachusetts.

In the twentieth and twenty-first centuries, many of America's black community leaders emerged from the church, business, and sport and entertainment, but they also sprang from Prince Hall Freemasonry with its combination of Enlightenment principles, spirituality, and mutuality. While the organization is predominantly African American, members have joined from other culturally diverse backgrounds.

> *The churches and the fraternal/mutual aid societies formed the core of black communities during the latter part of the eighteenth century. These institutions served as the staging ground for reform and protest organizations and were the foundation of the social and economic structure of black society. They were central to an African American sense of identity. Because there were few opportunities for blacks to participate in the wider society, political, social, and educational goals found an outlet in the institutions of the black community. These organizations became extremely important because they provided their members with mutual aid and protection, whether it was religious, cultural, social, recreational, physical, economic, or political.*

* * * *

THE DECLARATION OF INDEPENDENCE

The Declaration of Independence, the United States Constitution and the Constitutions of Freemasonry share many Enlightenment hallmarks with a common focus on freedom, justice, the separation of powers within a constitutional government, and religious tolerance. Indeed, 'no religious Test shall ever be required as a Qualification to any Office or public Trust under the United States'.

The Declaration of Independence is clear:

> *That all men are created equal, that they are endowed by their Creator with certain unalienable Rights, that among these are Life, Liberty and the pursuit of Happiness.*
>
> *—That to secure these rights, Governments are instituted among Men, deriving their just powers from the consent of the governed,*
>
> *—That whenever any Form of Government becomes destructive of these ends, it is the Right of the People to alter or to abolish it, and to institute new Government, laying its foundation on such principles and organizing its powers in such form, as to them shall seem most likely to effect their Safety and Happiness.*
>
> *Prudence, indeed, will dictate that Governments long established should not be changed for light and transient causes; and accordingly all experience hath shewn, that mankind are more disposed to suffer, while evils are sufferable, than to right themselves by abolishing the forms to which they are accustomed.*

Simón Bolívar
Ricardo Acevedo Bernal (1867 - 1930)

LATIN AMERICA

In 1733 the Grand Lodge of England appointed Randolph Tooke (1704-1765), a City merchant, to be Provincial Grand Master of South America. The appointment was honorific. Tooke, a member of Lodge No. 19 at the Queen's Arms in Newgate Street, London, represented the South Sea Company in Buenos Aires but there is no evidence that he constituted any Masonic Lodges.

Freemasonry developed in Latin America half-century later and spread across the continent in the nineteenth century, carried by European military and naval forces, as well as French, British (English and Scottish), Dutch and Irish merchants. It was also influenced by the United States.

It was also intertwined with the pro-Independence movements within Latin America.

Freemasonry's Enlightenment principles were part of an intellectual movement that spurred liberation. These ideals were shared by Latin Americans and their supporters in Europe, who included more than five thousand British volunteers who fought for the independence of the then Province of Colombia, some of whom formed Lodge Colombiana.

British volunteers were recruited in London chiefly by Luis Lopez Mendez, a Venezuelan lawyer based in Grafton Street, London. His house was purchased by the Government of Venezuela in 1978 and is now a museum and memorial to Francisco de Miranda.

Another Freemason, Jose de San Martín, was at the forefront of pro-independence movement in Argentina and Chile, as was Simón Bolívar, 'El Libertador', a Venezuelan soldier and politician who led the anti-colonial liberation movement in Venezuela, Colombia, Ecuador, Peru and Bolivia.

FRANCE

Although there is only limited documentation, it is accepted that two Paris Lodges were established in 1726 followed by four more in 1729, and that the movement quickly became widespread with lodges established in Valenciennes, Lyons, Rouen, Le Havre, Pau, Nantes, Caen, Bordeaux, Aubigny, Avignon, Montpelier, Marseilles and Bayonne. New degrees appeared shortly afterwards: the 'Scottish' or 'knightly' degrees.

Scots Master degrees had been worked in London in 1733, perhaps earlier, and the current balance of evidence suggests that higher degrees were created in France during the decade thereafter and developed further with still higher degrees. Current research suggests an interconnection between Scottish, Irish, English and French freemasonry during this period that can be linked to the creation of the Royal Arch degree. Given the personal connections between Europe's aristocrats, this should not be considered surprising.

French and other European aristocrats wished to embellish England's three-degree system. They preferred a system in which they could be raised to 'knights' or 'chevaliers', rather than be allegorically compared to stonemasons, an approach aligned with the medieval chivalric orders with which they were familiar.

Although it is hard to know precisely what influence freemasonry exerted on social and political developments in France, the speed with which it was adopted and the extent to which it spread suggest that its philosophical tenets had appeal.

The Duke of Richmond convened his first English lodge in France in 1734, the year that he succeeded as Duc d'Aubigny. Lodge meetings were held at Louise de Kérouaille, his grandmother's house on the Rue des Saints-Pères in Paris and in a private room at the Hôtel Bussy. Richmond also established a lodge at his grandmother's estate at Aubigny-sur-Nère, 40 kilometres south-east of Orléans.

The prelude to the Lodge meeting at Aubigny is recorded in a letter to Richmond dated 23 August 1734 from Thomas Hill, the duke's former tutor and now a friend and member of his household. Among other matters, it emphasises how Jean Theophilus Desaguliers altered the ritual – 'the production' – to create a 'greater air of antiquity and consequently make it more venerable' and thus more appealing to its aristocratic French audience:

> *I have communicated to the new, if I am not mistaken, right worshipful … Dr J Theophilus Desaguliers, your Grace's command relating to the brotherhood of Aubigny sur Nère. I need not tell you how pleased he is with this further propagation of masonry… When I mentioned the diploma he immediately asked me if I had not Amadis de Gaula or some of the old Romances. I was something surprised at his question, and begun to think as the house was tiled our brother had a mind to crack a joke. But it turned out quite otherwise. He only wanted to get a little of the vieux Gaulois in order to give his style the greater air of antiquity and consequently make it more venerable to the new lodge. He went from me fully intent on getting that or some other such book. What the production will be you may expect to see soon.*

It became customary for Richmond to travel to France annually and in September the following year he convened a lodge in Paris once again:

> *They write from Paris that His Grace the Duke of Richmond and the Rev. Dr Desaguliers (formerly Grand Masters of the Ancient and Honourable Society of Free and Accepted Masons and now authorised by the present Grand Master under his Hand and Seal, and the Seal of the Order) having called a lodge at the Hotel Bussy, His Excellency the Earl of Waldegrave, his Majesty's Ambassador to the French King; the Right Hon. the President Montesquieu; the Marquis de Lomaria; Lord Dursley, son of the Earl of Berkeley; the Hon. Mr Fitz-Williams;*

Messrs. Knight, father and son; Dr Hickman, and several other persons, both French and English, were present; and the following noblemen and gentlemen were admitted to the Order, viz., His Grace the Duke of Kingston; the Rt. Hon. the Count de St. Florentin, Secretary of State to his most Christian Majesty; the Right Hon. The Lord Chewton, son to the Earl of Waldegrave; Mr Pelham; Mr Herbert; Mr Armiger; Mr Cotton and Mr Clement. After which, the new Brethren gave a handsome Entertainment to all the Company.

The names and standing of those attending the Lodge underlines Freemasonry's status as a diplomatic tool. The central figure was the Comte de Saint-Florentin, a senior advisor to Louis XV and the minister responsible for the Huguenots in France. He would have been an appropriate figure to cultivate and the concurrent initiation of the Duke of Kingston and Earl Waldegrave's eldest son, James, Lord Chewton, would have flattered Phélypeaux much as the Duke of Newcastle's raising at Houghton Hall, Sir Robert Walpole's country house, had honoured the Duke of Lorraine a few years earlier.

A second key figure was President Montesquieu, Charles Louis de Secondat, Baron Montesquieu, president à mortier du parlement de Bordeaux. Among the other attendees, 'Mr Pelham' was Thomas Pelham Jr. (c.1705-1743), the Duke of Newcastle's loyal second cousin, MP for Hastings (1728-41). Pelham was at the time serving as Ambassador Waldegrave's private secretary.

One of France's most famous, albeit later, Masonic Lodges was the Lodge of the Neuf Soeurs (Nine Sisters or Nine Muses). It was established in Paris 1776 by Jérôme de Lalande, an Enlightenment scientist – an astronomer – who became its first master. The Lodge is notable for many reasons, including its prominent support for American Independence.

Lalande was followed in the chair by Benjamin Franklin (1779-81); the Marquis de La Salle (1781-83), an author and cavalry officer; Nicolas-Christiern de Thy, Compte de Milly (1783-84), an aristocrat, soldier and scientist, an associate of the French Royal Academy of Sciences; Charles Dupaty (1784), a painter and sculptor; Elie de Beaumont (1784-85), a celebrated lawyer; and Claude-Emmanuel de Pastoret (1788-89), an author, jurist, and Enlightenment politician.

One of its most famous members was Voltaire, initiated into the Lodge in 1778 towards the end of his life. Other members came from the aristocracy, the legal profession, the French Academy, or were politicians. Twelve were members of the Institut de France, which incorporated five académies, including the Académie Française.

The lodge ceased to operate as a Masonic lodge in 1790 and now operates as a Masonic research society.

THE NETHERLANDS

In March 1734 Prince William of Orange married the Princess Royal at St James's Palace in London. A few months later Vincent La Chapelle (c.1700-c.1746), joined their household and returned with them to The Hague as their chef de cuisine.

La Chapelle held a reputation as one of the most influential chefs in eighteenth-century Europe. He had been part of the household of Philip Stanhope, 4th Earl of Chesterfield, Britain's ambassador at The Hague, and subsequently that of the Count of Montijo, the Spanish envoy in London. La Chapelle was renowned as the author of the best-selling The Modern Cook and has more recently been described as an eighteenth-century Escoffier and a composite of Michel Roux, Heston Blumenthal and Gordon Ramsay.

La Chapelle was also an English Freemason and a Huguenot, a member of the lodge at the Rainbow Coffee House and of Prince Eugene's Head Coffee House. And he was a probable source for Britain's intelligence services. In that connection or otherwise, La Chapelle established the first domestic Masonic Lodge in the United

Provinces, Lodge 'L'Union Royale', at the Lion d'Or tavern at The Hague in November 1734, becoming its first master. Founder members included Phillipe Fluvet, senior warden, Daniel Friard, junior warden, and François Liégois, Salomon Noch, and Jean Fache. Four candidates were initiated at the first meeting: Antoine Maillet, the owner of the Lion d'Or; Louis Dagran, a cloth merchant; William Constant; and N. de St. Genevieve. The names suggest a Huguenot connection.

Louis Dagran's journal, Annales et Archives des Francs-Macons, indicates that the Duke of Richmond was involved with the Lodge's foundation. On 22 November 1734, François Liégois, one of the Duke's former employees, asked for the duke's help to obtain a warrant – 'a legitimate constitution' – from the Grand Lodge of England. The warrant was forthcoming, despatched from London in March 1735 and accompanied by a copy of the 1723 Constitutions.

A second lodge, 'Le Véritable Zèle', was consecrated at The Hague a year later in October 1735 with Dagran as its first master. The event was noted in Amsterdamsche Saturdagsche Courant on 3 November 1735, which recorded that the Treasurer General, Johan Cornelis Rademacher, had been made Grand Master of the United Provinces. The lodge afterwards took the name 'Loge du Grand Maître des Provinces Unies et du Ressort de la Généralité'.

The initial reaction to such an announcement was suspicion. Fearing that improper influence might be exerted and wary of its Enlightenment ideas which clashed with those of the political establishment, especially the church, the Dutch provinces lobbied for freemasonry to be proscribed, an interdiction that lasted from 1740-44, albeit that it was enforced only loosely.

In 1756 ten Dutch lodges joined to form the Grand Lodge of the Netherlands: 'Groote Loge der Zeven Vereenigde Nederlanden'. The name was changed in 1817 to the Grand Orient of the Netherlands.

Two princes from the House of Orange held the position of Grand Master of Freemasons in the nineteenth century: Prince Frederik, the younger brother of King William II (who was also a Freemason), from 1816-81; and Prince Alexander, the youngest son of King William III, from 1882 until his death in 1884.

In the later eighteenth and throughout the nineteenth century, colonialism and the military carried Dutch Freemasonry to the Antilles, Surinam, Ceylon, India, Southern Africa, the Dutch East Indies, Brazil and China. Some Lodges endured and there are today around sixteen non-domestic Lodges under the jurisdiction of the Grand Orient of the Netherlands.

GERMANY & AUSTRIA

Prior to the late eighteenth century Germany comprised numerous independent states – electorates – that formed part of the Holy Roman Empire. Cologne, Mainz and Triers were ecclesiastical electorates ruled by bishops; and Brandenburg, Bavaria, Hanover, Saxony, Wurtemburg and the Kingdom of Bohemia were presided over by dukes or princes. The two largest states were Austria and Prussia, who vied for leadership. Political and economic priorities differed among the various states, as did religious affiliations. Those in the north-west and south-east were mainly Catholic, and those in the north-east and south-west predominantly Protestant.

The Holy Roman Empire of which they were part had been led since the mid-fifteenth century by the male head of the Austrian House of Habsburg. But while the Holy Roman Emperor had influence he had limited formal authority and in that sense, as Voltaire commented, the Holy Roman Empire was 'neither holy, nor Roman nor an empire'.

Freemasonry was established in Hamburg in the 1720s by merchant traders and expanded south and west in the decades that followed. William Preston wrote that the Earl of Strathmore granted a deputation for a lodge in Hamburg in 1733 and there is evidence of another lodge meeting there in the later 1730s under an English Provincial Grand Master for Prussia and Brandenburg. This may have evolved into Lodge Absalom which was warranted on 23 October 1740. It was common practice for overseas lodges to be warranted by the Grand Lodge of England some years after their establishment. Lodge Absalom subsequently chartered daughter Lodges in Brunswick (1744), Hanover (1746), Celle (1748), Oldenburg (1752), Schwerin (1754), and Hildesheim (1762).

Lodge Union of Frankfurt was established at Frankfurt-on-Main in 1742. And although most, perhaps two-thirds or more of German Lodges later adopted other forms of Masonic ritual, principally 'Rectified' or 'Strict Observance', and later Swedish Rite, Lodge Union was one of a small number that continued to adhere to the English system of three Craft degrees.

In September 1740, the year he became king, Frederick the Great (1712-1786), authorized the formation of a Lodge in Berlin. This was The Three Globes; it became the de facto Prussian Grand Lodge.

For much of the first half of the eighteenth century, Germany followed France's lead in the arts and philosophy. French was also the language of diplomacy and of elite polite society. And as France gradually adopted Enlightenment tenets, Germany followed suit with its own version, the 'Aufklärung', which altered Germany's intellectual culture, affecting German art, music, philosophy and science.

Gotthold Ephraim Lessing (1729-1781) was at the core of the German Enlightenment from 1751 in his role as editor of the Berlin Gazette. His circle included Friedrich Nicolai (1733-1811) and Moses Mendelssohn (1729-1786), with whom Lessing collaborated in the authorship of *Pope – ein Metaphysiker*!

Lessing's *Nathan the Wise*, his last major work, debated personal morality and explored issues such as religious toleration: 'where Christian, Jew and Muslim can unite as one – a dream that is so sweet'. Lessing was initiated into freemasonry in lodge Zu den Drie Goldenen Rosen in Hamburg in 1771.

Other German Enlightenment figures reshaping German culture who are known or believed to have been freemasons include Wilhelm von Humboldt (1767-1835); Friedrich Schleiermacher (1768-1834); Johann Wolfgang von Goethe (1749-1832); Friedrich Wilhelm Schiller (1775-1854); and Johann Gottfried von Herder (1744-1803). Von Herde, a friend of Immanuel Kant and Johann Goethe, an intellectual innovator, was one of the leaders of Germany's proto-Romantic Sturm und Drang movement. He was initiated in 1766 in Lodge Zur in Riga. Goethe was initiated in Amalia Lodge at Weimar in June 1780.

Music was at the heart of the German and Austrian Enlightenment and strongly supported by the elites, many of whom were freemasons. Three of the Esterházy family's directors of music or 'kapellmeisters' – Joseph Haydn, Paul Wranitzky and Ignaz Pleyel – performed in Lodge meetings. Haydn initiated into Zur wahren Eintracht; Wranitzky into Zur gekronten Hoffnung; and Pleyel into an unnamed lodge in Eberau, Hungary. However the best-known composer associated with Austrian Freemasonry was Wolfgang Amadeus Mozart, initiated in 1784 into Lodge Zur Wohltätigkeit.

SWEDEN

Swedish merchants and members of the Swedish nobility were introduced to Freemasonry in Paris in the 1730s. Villeroy-Coustos Lodge, an English lodge, had at least seven members who were Swedish, including Count Carl Fredrik Scheffer (1715-86), a diplomat and politician, and subsequently Grand Master of Sweden (1753-74). Other Scandinavian members included Niels Krabbe De Wind, Denmark's Ambassador to Paris, and Carl Adolph von Plessen, one of his colleagues at the Danish Embassy.

Swedish Freemasonry was sponsored by Charles Radcliffe, the titular 5th Earl of Derwentwater, a Jacobite exile resident in France. As Grand Master of Freemasons in France, Derwentwater issued a charter to Carl Fredrik Scheffer permitting him to establish Lodges in Sweden and setting out Masonic regulations – 'Règles générales de la Maçonnerie' – based on the 1723 Constitutions.

Swedish Rite Freemasonry developed in the second half of the eighteenth century and has remained virtually unchanged since that time. Its ceremonies are based on a combination of eighteenth-century Scottish and French Masonic ritual, both having roots in and similarities to English ritual, as well as elements of Rosicrucianism.

Unlike English and other Anglo-Saxon Masonic ritual, Swedish Rite is open exclusively to those of the Christian faith.

Swedish Rite contains ten principal degrees compared to the three 'blue' degrees of English Craft Freemasonry and the fourth 'red' or Royal Arch degree. It begins with three St John's Craft degrees, progresses through two St Andrew's or Scottish degrees, and is followed by five Chapter or Templar degrees. Members of the Grand Council of Swedish Rite take an eleventh degree, becoming Knight Commanders of the Red Cross.

Swedish Rite is based on the concept of personal spiritual advancement and progression through the degrees takes place over an extended period of a decade or more. Moving from a St John's lodge to a St Andrew's lodge through to Chapter is not automatic and does not mirror the English pattern of an ascending order of offices within a Lodge from inner guard to junior deacon, senior deacon, junior warden, senior warden, and master.

The first five degrees in Swedish Rite are broadly similar to the first four in English freemasonry, but there are differences. One is that each degree has its own bespoke lodge room that sets the Masonic tone and throws into relief the moral and spiritual aspects of that degree. Formal court dress (now 'white tie'), and a sword and scabbard are worn by all participants throughout each ceremony.

Swedish Rite embodies individual spiritual and moral advancement. The degrees are not open and secrecy is maintained conscientiously in order to preserve the emotional impact for each participant. A candidate's development is marked by and taught via a series of one-act morality plays, with the allegorical aspects of the degree explained through lectures and catechisms in which formal answers are given by the candidate to set questions. The ambiance and formality are designed to focus the attention of the candidate on the intrinsic message of the ceremony.

DENMARK & NORWAY

When Freemasonry arrived in Scandinavia in the middle of the eighteenth century, Denmark and Norway constituted a dual monarchy and their early Masonic histories are thus intertwined. While Freemasonry was brought to Sweden from France through noblemen and diplomats, the first Masonic activities in Denmark and later Norway came from the Northern German states via civil servants, officers and merchants.

The difference in origins combined with sparse inter-Scandinavian Masonic contact suggests that Freemasonry in Denmark and Norway on the one side, and Sweden on the other, followed different traditions during the formative years. Consequently, the Craft, and to an even wider extent, the additional degrees, evolved in separate ways in the two regions.

Freemasonry arrived in Denmark when five Master Masons met in Copenhagen on 11 November 1743 and founded a lodge which would later be named St Martin. Of the five founders, four had been initiated in Hamburg, and one in Berlin.

The following year, brethren from St Martin left to establish another lodge which obtained a constitution from the Grand Lodge in London in 1745 and exists to this day under the name Zorobabel og Frederik til det kronede Haab (i.e., Zorobabel and Frederick of the Crowned Hope, colloquially known as Z&F), the oldest Masonic lodge in operation in the Nordic countries. At this time the lodges worked a German variant of English ritual.

A Provincial Grand Master for Denmark and Norway, Count Christian Conrad Danneskiold-Laurvig, was appointed by the Grand Lodge in London in 1749, and the Craft in the dual monarchy was formally subordinate to England until 1765. Three more lodges were established during the first two decades of Danish Freemasonry, as well as three lodges working the Scottish Master's degree, and a lodge of adoption. Rosa's adaptation of the Clermont system was also present in Copenhagen from 1762 to 1764 in form of the chapter Capitulum Hafniense.

Circumstantial evidence suggest that the first Norwegian lodge was consecrated in Christiania (present-day Oslo) by the Provincial Grand Master Count Danneskiold-Laurvig during the summer months of 1749. This was probably never reported back to London since no relevant records are present in the English archives. Minutes from the lodge is extant from 1757 and indicate that the work was suspended for several long periods.

PORTUGAL AND SPAIN

In 1738 Pope Clement XII published a Papal Bull sanctioning freemasonry and freemasons. Taking his lead from Rome, Philip V prohibited freemasonry in Spain in 1740, issuing a decree that those deemed freemasons would be condemned to the galleys. Portugal followed suit with a similar proscription, albeit that an English Masonic lodge had been established in Lisbon in 1735 by British merchants who enjoyed the implied protection of the Royal Navy:

> *They write from Lisbon, that by Authority of the Right Hon. The Earl of Weymouth, the then Grand Master of all Mason Lodges, Mr George Gordon, Mathematician, has constituted a Lodge of free and accepted*

Masons in that City; and that a great many Merchants of the factory, and other people of distinction, have been received and regularly made Free Masons; that Lord George Graham, Lord Forrester, and a great many other gentlemen belonging to the English Fleet, being Brethren, were present at constituting the lodge; and 'tis expected that in a short time it will be one of the greatest abroad.

In 1741 John Coustos, a diamond dealer, a member of the Huguenot lodge at Prince Eugene's Head Coffee House in St Alban's Street, London, and the founder of Villeroy-Coustos Lodge in Paris, established a Lodge in Lisbon. Shortly afterwards he was betrayed to the Inquisition and accused of heresy. Arrested and tortured, Coustos claimed that he was unaware that freemasonry had been prohibited in Portugal and, in any event, that the lodge had met at 'private houses of chosen friends' and not in public. Despite his protestations, Coustos was found guilty and sentenced to five years in the galleys.

Coustos nonetheless managed to get a message to John Barbut, his brother-in-law, a well-placed government official in London, and British diplomatic pressure was exerted to secure Coustos's release:

The Earl of Harrington was so good as to endeavour to procure my freedom [and] spoke to his grace the Duke of Newcastle... with a view to supplicate for leave from our sovereign that his minister at Lisbon might demand me as a subject of Great Britain. His Majesty interposing in my favour and his commands being dispatched to Mr Compton, the British minister at Lisbon, that gentleman demanded my liberty of the king of Portugal, in his Britannic Majesty's name, which I accordingly obtained the latter end of October, 1744.

The Earl of Harrington was Secretary of State for the Northern Department; the Duke of Newcastle, Secretary of State for the Southern Department and responsible for diplomatic relations with

Portugal. Harrington was a freemason, as was his brother, Charles Stanhope, and his cousin, Lord Chesterfield, as was Newcastle.

Following his return to England, Coustos wrote *Sufferings* setting out his experience at the hands of the Inquisition and containing 'Copper Plates descriptive of the Tortures he endured'. Published in 1746 and dedicated to Harrington and Newcastle, the book was edited before publication, probably at Newcastle's behest, with additional anti-Catholic material included so that it could fulfil a propagandist role in the wake of the 1745 Jacobite Rising.

English Masonic Lodges in Portugal were followed by Irish and French Lodges. But domestic Portuguese freemasonry began only in the nineteenth century. In 1802 in agreement with the Grand Orient of France, a Lusitanian Grand Orient was formed and recognized soon after by the Antients' Grand Lodge in England. It continues to be recognized by the Grand Orient of France and is part of a continental European Masonic tradition which invokes liberty of conscience. A second Portuguese Grand Lodge, the Grande Loja Legal de Portugal, was founded in 1991 and is recognised by the United Grand Lodge of England, the Grand Lodges of Ireland and Scotland, and other Anglo-Saxon grand lodges. English Masonic lodges are also present in Portugal operating under the direct supervision of UGLE.

ITALY

Italy, like Germany, was in the eighteenth century a patchwork of independent kingdoms, republics, duchies and the Papal States. Although press censorship was relatively strict and the Inquisition retained influence, there was nonetheless an intellectual climate that was open to new ideas and within the numerous universities and academies and among the educated elites many were receptive to the rational and sceptical ideas advanced by Enlightenment thinkers. And while it might have been anticipated that the spread of Freemasonry in a Catholic country would be constrained, as was the case in Spain and Portugal, this was less the position in Italy.

It is understood that Freemasonry was introduced to Italy in the early 1730s and that a Masonic lodge was operating in Florence by 1733, if not earlier. Harry Carr in *The Freemason At Work* argues that a Lodge in Florence was instituted by Lionel Sackville, Earl of Middlesex (created Duke of Dorset in 1720), without a warrant from the Grand Lodge of England, something borne out by John Lane's *Masonic Records*. And following its success, other Lodges were established in Milan, Verona, Padua, Vincenza, Venice and Naples.

A significant factor behind Masonic expansion in Italy may have been the relatively large numbers of British aristocrats on the Grand Tour. The publicity that this generated, the manner in which the Craft was spreading elsewhere in Europe among the elites, especially in France, and the initiation of the Duke of Lorraine (later the Duke of Tuscany) in 1731, underlay Pope Clement XII's decision to issue a Bull against Freemasonry in 1738.

The stated objective was 'to block the broad road that the influence of the Society might open to the uncorrected commission of sin'. The faithful were thus forbidden 'to enter, propagate or support the Freemasons... or to help them in any way, openly or in secret, directly or indirectly... or to be present at any of their meetings, under pain of excommunication.'

Some consider *In Eminenti* and later papal Bulls to be a continuation of the Counter Reformation. After all, Freemasonry, in the eyes of the Catholic Church, was a movement developed by Protestant heretics. That it appealed to Protestants and Catholics, and to other faiths, and had a growing membership, was of concern given that its approach to religion marginalised the role of the Catholic Church as the sole path to spiritual redemption.

From Rome's standpoint, Freemasonry had to be curtailed or, at a minimum, Catholics prohibited from joining the organization since it accepted members of all faiths and required only a belief in a Supreme Being. That the ban was widely ignored in Italy, even after the second Bull in 1751, suggests that Freemasonry's Enlightenment tenets and fraternal sociability had garnered widespread appeal.

As a footnote, it is interesting to note that the unification of Italy (bar the Papal States) was completed in 1860/61 under the leadership of Giuseppe Garibaldi, an Italian nationalist and Freemason who had previously fought in Latin America in favour of democratic republicanism. Garibaldi was initiated into Freemasonry in L'Asil de la Vertud Lodge in Montevideo in 1844 and came to see Freemasonry – stripped of its more esoteric elements – as a network that could unite progressive liberal men as brothers, nationally and internationally. In 1862 Italy's Supreme Council of the Ancient and Accepted Scottish Rite, a forum for Italian Freemasons with radical republican views, made him Grand Master. Two years later, the Grand Orient of Italy convening in Florence also elected Garibaldi Grand Master; he served one term in office.

Garibaldi travelled to Britain in April 1864 where his popularity stretched from the masses to the elites. Greeted by adoring crowds, he had an audience with the Prince of Wales and was hosted by the aristocracy but also met with European exiles.

Freemasons responded positively to his visit. Garibaldi received a deputation from Polish National Lodge, No. 534, led by the artist Sigismund Rosenthal, its Master. The Lodge had been formed by exiled Polish revolutionaries banished during the Insurrections of 1830 and 1846. The Lodge jewel, presented to Garibaldi, is the Polish Eagle mounted on a cross appended to a blue and black ribbon, the colours of the Polish Virtuti Miliari. Garibaldi was also invited to a meeting of Salisbury Lodge, No. 435, in Soho, London, where he was granted honorary membership; it was accepted on his behalf by Giuseppe Basile, a senior member of Garibaldi's entourage.

INDIA

Freemasonry was brought to India by members of the British East India Company with the first Lodge established under the jurisdiction of the Grand Lodge of England – No. 72 – consecrated in 1728 at Fort William, Calcutta, Bengal. The following year, 1729, Captain Ralph Farwinter was appointed Provisional Grand Master for East India. A Provincial Grand Lodge was established in Madras in 1752 and a Provincial Grand Lodge in Bombay in 1758.

Other countries and Masonic jurisdictions also established Lodges in India. Those under the Irish Constitution were the product of travelling regimental lodges. Scottish Constitution lodges appear at the beginning of the nineteenth century as a function of trade and the military. But at least three other constitutions were also present: Lodge Solomon was founded in 1758 at Tandelga, Bengal, under the Dutch Constitution by the Commander-of-the-Fleet of the Netherlands East India Company; a French Constitution lodge, Sincere Amité, was chartered at Pondicherry in 1787; and in 1807 Lodge de l'amour Fraternelle was founded at Tranquebar in Tamil Nadu with a warrant granted by the National Grand Lodge of Denmark.

The first recorded Indian freemason was a Muslim, Umdat-ul-Umara, the future Nawab of Arcot. He was initiated in 1775 in Lodge Perfect Unanimity, Madras, and after his initiation stated that he considered the title of an English Mason to be 'at once a cement to the friendship between your nation and me and confirms me the friend of mankind'. He expanded on the sentiment in a letter to the Grand Master of England in 1778:

> *An early knowledge and participation of the benefits arising to our house from its intimate union of councils and interests with the British nation and a deep veneration for the laws, constitutions and manners of the latter, have for many years of my life led me to seize every opportunity of drawing the ties subsisting between us closer*

> *and closer. By the accounts which have reached me of the principles and practices of your Fraternity, nothing can be more pleasing to the Sovereign Ruler of the Universe, who we all, though in different ways, adore, or more honourable to His creatures, for they stand upon the broad basis of indiscriminate and universal benevolence. Under this conviction I have long wished to be admitted of your Fraternity; and now that I am initiated, I consider the title of an English Mason as one of the most honourable I possess.*

India underwent substantial change under British rule, not all of which was beneficial. But Freemasonry with its emphasis on fraternity and brotherly relief and a symbolism that had parallels with Eastern faiths, attracted the interest of many educated Indians living in Bombay and Calcutta, in particular members of the Zoroastrian community.

By the 1840s a minority of British Freemasons were seeking to recruit Indians into the Craft, but they met resistance. In Bengal, for example, by-law 55 of the Provincial Grand Lodge prevented Indians from admission and it was not until 1872 that the first Hindu, a Bro. P. C. Dutt, was admitted to Lodge Anchor & Hope, and then only after nine years of blackballing and appeals. In Bombay, however, matters moved more positively and more rapidly with the consequence that, after some effort, Lodge Rising Star of Western India was formed in 1843 as the first Masonic lodge open to those not of European origin.

Lodge Rising Star of Western India was established following an application in 1840 by Maneckjee Cursetjee, a citizen of Bombay, to Lodge Perseverance, No. 546, then under the English Constitution. Following his rejection on grounds of race, Maneckjee petitioned the Duke of Sussex, the Grand Master of UGLE. The duke ruled that it was improper to discriminate and that Maneckjee should be admitted to Freemasonry.

Two years after its formation, Lodge Rising Star had sixty members and ended its third year with a further seventeen. Other lodges followed and accepted non-European members in the 1850s. Hindus and Sikhs also joined freemasonry and in the following years the Bhagavad Gita and Granth Sahib were placed on the altar.

The Lodge provided a unique environment in which Indians of different religions and communities and Indians and Europeans could interact. Freemasonry may not have been the only movement that spread the principle of friendship and unity across sectarian and class lines but it was probably one of the more effective. Admittedly, the Craft's success in fostering fraternal bonds across doctrinal divides also served colonial purposes by 'bringing together men of every rank and station, annihilating prejudices of creed and profession, reconciling opposite temperaments, and cultivating good will and brotherly love'.

Freemasonry provided an escape valve in an otherwise highly structured colonial culture, enabling Indians to be 'citizens of Empire', achieve brotherhood with the British, and bring together different communities:

> *high and low, rich and poor, member and visitor meet in a fraternal manner that magnetizes and knits heart to heart, and forms friendships and establishes connections never to be broken.*

In 1867, the Master of Lodge Rising Star of Western India, Rustomjee Bahadurjee, declared that:

> *Freemasonry is spread all over the world, but in India she has special ends to accomplish. If at this moment there is any institution which is calculated to unite the governing and the governed in a bond of friendship and brotherhood, it is, I humbly submit, this institution, and hence this Lodge, which is specially for the benefit of the Natives, holds a position peculiar to itself.*

A decade later in 1877, K. R. Cama, a leading merchant and fellow lodge member, commented similarly:

> *It is hard to think of any other institution in India at the time that had the power to effect such social cohesion between the races and, for the British, to contribute to imperial consolidation among the more influential members of the colonized community.*

Freemasonry also influenced India's independence movement. Half the Presidents of the India National Congress were freemasons, including Dadabhai Naoroji, 'the Grand Old Man of India', a founding member of London's Marquis of Dalhousie Lodge, No. 1159, its first Secretary (1867–71) and later its Master (1871-72).

Dadabhai was a founder of the Indian National Congress in Bombay in 1885, elected its President in 1886 and again in 1893 and 1906, and a mentor to a younger generation of nationalist leaders including Gopal Krishna Gokhale, Mohandas Gandhi and Muhammed Ali Jinnah. Dadabhai was also elected to the British Parliament in 1892, the first non-white person to become an MP, from where he argued strongly in favour of reform.

* * * *

AFTERWORD

By the late 1720s, English Freemasonry had become one of - if not the - most attractive yet accessible destinations for the aristocracy, gentry and aspirational more widely. And Grand Lodge and English Freemasonry's more eminent constituent lodges were led by a parade of noble Grand Masters from John, Duke of Montagu, to Thomas, Duke of Norfolk, Earl Marshal of England.

Freemasonry had been positioned intentionally at the pinnacle of Hanoverian society, and Desaguliers and his colleagues deployed its celebrated social, philosophical and intellectual connections to cement an alliance with the British establishment.

For some three decades through to the mid-eighteenth century, the leadership at Grand Lodge was motivated by a powerful desire to support and safeguard the Hanoverian succession. Those at its centre believed it to be essential that Britain remain a bulwark against both Jacobitism and the risk of encroachment by continental Europe's absolutist monarchies.

As a measure of its achievement, the number of lodges within the jurisdiction of the Grand Lodge of England increased from the founding four in 1717 to over sixty in 1725, more than one hundred in 1730 and around two hundred in 1740. Although some lodges failed to survive, by the mid-1730s Freemasonry under the jurisdiction of the Grand Lodge of England had a presence throughout London and across provincial England and Wales.

Lodges were also established internationally, from the eastern seaboard of the Americas including Boston, New York, Philadelphia, Charles Town and Savannah, across continental Europe from Lisbon to Vienna and St Petersburg, and as far east as Bengal in India.

1725 List of Lodges
Engraved by John Pine

To look back to the publication of the Constitutions in 1723 just a few years after the founding of the first Grand Lodge of England in 1717 is an opportunity to reflect on the threads that gave rise to those events and created the foundations on which Modern Freemasonry rests today.

* * * *

THE

CONSTITUTIONS

OF THE

FREE-MASONS.

CONTAINING THE

Hiſtory, Charges, Regulations, &c. of that moſt Ancient and Right Worſhipful *FRATERNITY.*

For the Uſe of the LODGES.

LONDON:

Printed by WILLIAM HUNTER, for JOHN SENEX at the *Globe,* and JOHN HOOKE at the *Flower-de-luce* over-againſt *St. Dunſtan's Church,* in *Fleet-ſtreet.*

In the Year of Maſonry —— 5723
Anno Domini —— 1723

Bought Anno Domini — 1769
Christ born Anno Mundi — 4004
5773

The Constitutions of the Free-Masons

THE CONSTITUTIONS
A LONG EIGHTEENTH-CENTURY TIMELINE

1723	Constitutions (Hooke & Senex, London)
1730	Constitutions (J. Pennell, Dublin, Ireland)
1730	*De instillingen, historien... reglelmenten...* (Cornelius van Zantem, Gravenhague, Netherlands) [Dutch edition, trans. Johan Kuenen]
1731	Constitutions (B. Creake, London)
1734	Constitutions (B. Franklin, Philadelphia, PA)
1735	*A Pocket Companion* (William Smith, London) [including pirated parts of 1723 Constitutions]
1735	*A Pocket Companion* (William Smith, Dublin). [pirated as above]
1736	Constitutions (The Hague, Netherlands) [French-language version of Kuenen's translation]
1738	Constitutions (J. Anderson, London)
1741	Constitutions (Frankfurt) [German-language translation based on Kuenen]
1751	Constitutions (E. Spratt, Dublin, Ireland)
1754	Constitutions (J. Entick, London)
1756	Constitutions (J. Entick, London)
1756	Ahiman Rezon (L. Dermott, London)
1764	Ahiman Rezon (L. Dermott, London)
1765	Constitutions (J. Entick, London)
1767	Constitutions (J. Entick, London)
1769	Constitutions (G. Kearsley, London)
1778	Ahiman Rezon (L. Dermott, London)
1780	Ahiman Rezon (L. Dermott, London)
1782	Ahiman Rezon (L. Dermott, London)
1783	Constitutions (Grand Lodge of Pennsylvania)

1783	*Rules and Regulations of the Grand Lodge of Massachusetts* (Boston)
1784	Constitutions (J. Noorthouck, London)
1785	Constitutions (Grand Lodge of New York)
1787	Constitutions (Lodge #190 Antients, Charleston, SC)
1787	Ahiman Rezon (L. Dermott, London)
1789	Constitutions (Grand Lodge of Connecticut)
1789	Constitutions (Grand Lodge of New York)
1789	Regulations (Grand Lodge of Virginia)
1790	Regulations (Grand Lodge of New Jersey)
1790	Regulations (Grand Lodge of Pennsylvania)
1791	Constitutions (Grand Lodge of Virginia)
1791	Regulations (Grand Lodge of South Carolina)
1792	Constitutions (I. Thomas, Worcester, MA, USA)
1792	Regulations (Grand Lodge of New Hampshire)
1797	Ahiman Rezon (L. Dermott, London)
1797	Constitutions (Grand Lodge of Maryland)
1836	Constitutions (Grand Lodge of Scotland)

THE AUTHOR

Dr Richard (Ric) Berman is a British historian. He has written a series of books that place eighteenth-century English, Irish and American Freemasonry within a social and political context including *The Foundations of Modern Freemasonry*, a study of the political and religious rationale behind the creation of the first Grand Lodge, and *The Grand Lodge of England & Colonial America: America's Grand Masters*, illustrating America's early Grand Masters. He has also written numerous papers for academic and Masonic journals.

A freemason for over forty years, Dr Berman is a Past Master of Quatuor Coronati Lodge, the premier lodge of Masonic research, and PM of two other English Lodges. He holds Grand Rank in the United Grand Lodge of England and is also an American Freemason, a member of Fiat Lux, #1717, in Washington D.C.

Dr Berman was awarded his Doctorate in History from the University of Exeter and a Master of Arts from the University of Cambridge, where he read Economics. His postdoctoral research took place at the University of Oxford's Modern European History Research Centre.

Dr Berman is a Visiting Research Fellow at Oxford Brookes University, a Fellow of the Royal Historical Society and a Life Fellow of the Huguenot Society.

* * * *

Frontispiece
1756 Constitutions

Frontispiece
1784 Constitutions

INDEX

UNITED GRAND LODGE
OF ENGLAND

The Old Stables Press
• Oxfordshire •

Printed in Great Britain
by Amazon

84897505R00092